THROWN
ON AN E-BIKE

(What Could Possibly Go Wrong)

GLENN REDDICK

Three Months on an E-Bike
Copyright © 2021 by Glenn Reddick

All rights reserved. No part of this publication may be reproduced, distributed, or transmitted in any form or by any means, including photocopying, recording, or other electronic or mechanical methods, without the prior written permission of the author, except in the case of brief quotations embodied in critical reviews and certain other non-commercial uses permitted by copyright law.

Tellwell Talent
www.tellwell.ca

ISBN
978-0-2288-5806-5 (Paperback)
978-0-2288-5807-2 (eBook)

Table of Contents

About this Book v
1. You've Got To Be Kidding 1
2. Snakes Alive 14
3. A Short Cut To A Stampede 21
4. The Railway and a Cheeky Wallaby 25
5. The Wild Southwest 30
6. When It Rains, It Pours 41
7. Cuts and Bruises 47
8. Rona and La Niña Buddy Up 54
9. Enter Neville the Chihuahua 62
10. On the Road Again 68
11. Riding the Breeze 75
12. Oh No… My Wallet 83
13. Two-Wheeled Weekends 89
14. Distractions and Brownie Points 95
15. The Challenges of the Long Weekend in March 102
16. Into the Light 113
17. Rituals and Relief 119
18. Holidays 127
19. Done and Dusted 141

References 151

About this Book

The hilarious reactions from my friends, family and colleagues when I told them about my adventures riding my new e-bike to work for three months convinced me to write this book. My misadventures became a topic of conversation each day at work. Typical questions included:

"How was the ride today?"

"Chased by anything lately?"

I decided to change the names of some of the characters so as not to offend anybody, but the events certainly happened. I wrote the stories over the three-month period I was riding to work and around the area. Writing this book was a great distraction and gave me something different to do on weekends and evenings. It is my first attempt at writing a book, and other books may follow, you never know. I really enjoyed writing it and hope you enjoy reading it.

I hope this book encourages you to get out there, enjoy nature and possibly visit some of the places I wrote about. I live in a beautiful part of Australia, and if you decide to ride along the rail trail in the story you will see some of the things I mention in this book first-hand.

There are a lot of people to thank who supported me and encouraged me to write it down, and without them I would never have done it. In particular, I would like to thank my partner Jo for putting up with me. Thanks also to local artist Caroline Healey, who brought the book to life with her cover design and the beautifully illustrated map of the area.

1

You've Got To Be Kidding

I wouldn't exactly describe myself as a hoon driver; funnily enough, I'm not actually fond of driving fast. It is true, however, that I am afflicted with legendary impatience. As an Aries, impatience is probably my most identifiable character trait. My good mate, another Glenn, used to say "Curse your Arian impatience."

This is probably the root cause of what happened next.

It seemed a normal day just like any other, except that it wasn't. Staring into the eyes of the two traffic officers I saw one thing in their collective demeanour: punishment! I hardly ever speed when I'm driving. Well, OK, sometimes. So you can imagine my surprise that on the morning of December 23, 2020, my car was pulled over for speeding.

It is true that I was in a hurry with Christmas holidays fast approaching and much to finish at work before the office closed for the break. I also took a different route than usual to avoid the many sets of traffic lights on the way to save time.

"Do you know the speed limit here, Sir?"

"Um, 70, 60?" I suggested optimistically.

There were no speed limit signs, and this was on the very outskirts of Warrnambool with a row of houses on one side and farmland on the other.

"No sir, it is 50, and we have clocked your speed at 78." My heart sank.

"You've got to be kidding," I said.

"Oh no, Sir," they replied politely in stereo, "We are definitely not kidding."

And they weren't.

If you exceed the speed limit by more than 25 km/h in the state of Victoria, you're assessed an automatic three-month licence suspension. Automatic!

When the officers asked if there was anything I wanted to say, which they advised would be recorded, I resisted the temptation to give them a quick rendition of "Jingle Bells," in the hope it may change the outcome. It was nearly Christmas, and I thought I could prevail upon the spirit of the holidays. Thinking the better of it, I said nothing and drove away without possibly being arrested.

The licence suspension was dated to start in January, so at least I had some time to think, make arrangements and plan.

So at the end of the already awful COVID-19 year that was 2020, I was faced with another unexpected challenge: how to manage my eighteen-kilometre commute from rural Koroit to coastal Warrnambool and back... without a car. Hmm!

In case you don't know the area, Warrnambool is a town of approximately thirty-five thousand residents situated in the southwest corner of the state of Victoria, southern Australia. Known as Windy Warrnambool, the weather is changeable to say the least! Koroit is a lot smaller at a touch over two thousand inhabitants and is a little inland to the northwest. The other place in this story is Port Fairy, a quaint fishing village twenty-eight kilometres from Warrnambool.

I work for the local council, and I was classified by the government as an essential worker during the coronavirus pandemic. Although I worked from home regularly at the height of the pandemic, I was still required to go into the office several times per week. Not being able to drive was going to be a big problem.

I must be one of the few people who actually likes working from home. Most people initially enjoyed it, but the novelty wore off and they missed the face-to-face human interaction. Not so for me; I got so much more done without the endless distractions of being in an office environment, and I could put a load of washing on between video meetings, phone calls and endless emails. Maybe it is also because I'm a miserable git! As the pandemic seemed to be more or less managed in Australia by December 2020, there was an increasing need and expectation to be in the office. I was also working with a new director whom I wanted to get to know so he could fully understand my role.

So working from home every day was not an option. I simply had to come up with a solution as to how to get to the office and back. Walk? C'mon, be serious. Run? Hardly. I'll quietly mention that I hadn't been on a bike very much in thirty years, and my fifty-something physique doesn't much resemble the rippling finesse of my youth, so a bike seemed a remote option as well. There was always the bus, but I wasn't keen in the middle of a pandemic. I could have asked my workmates who live nearby for a lift, but I'm quite independent and hate imposing on people. Besides, this was my problem and it was up to me to resolve it somehow. Getting a lift from my partner Jo wasn't really an option as she worked most days, left very early and travelled in the opposite direction. It was completely impractical to ask her for a lift.

Then it suddenly came to me. *I've got it! I'll ride the e-bike down the rail trail!* The rail trail particularly appealed because, being something of an out of practice cyclist, I didn't fancy the prospect of riding on busy roads. The rail trail is a disused rail corridor which has been cleverly converted into a cycle and walking path that passes through Koroit and connects Warrnambool to Port Fairy. It traverses a distance of some thirty-seven kilometres, with the Koroit to Warrnambool section stretching 18.4 km, a distance that might just be possible to commute each day by bike.

Yes, that's it. Can't be that hard. The weather's good this time of year, and it's only three months—twelve weeks—not bad if you say it quickly! At least I could retain a degree of independence and dignity as well.

Although it sounded like an easy solution on the surface, there were some issues I'd obviously need to work through like the possibility of bad weather, bike breakdowns, poisonous snakes, not to mention staying on the damn thing. However, along with being impatient, I'm also known for skimming over the minor details; I'm more of a blue sky thinker sort of chap. What could possibly go wrong? Hey, I might even like it. Get fit, lose a few of those COVID-19 pounds I accumulated through working from home and being in lockdown.

With steely resolve I set about breaking the news to my partner Jo with an airy sense of optimism. This was going to be awkward. *OK, here goes*, I thought. The telephone conversation went something like this:

"Are you sitting down at the moment?" I asked.

"WHY...?"

"Well, you see, here's the thing... I've just lost my licence for three months for speeding."

Silence. I could almost hear her mind taking it in. Then, like a wave, it broke.

"I told you this would happen. What are you going to do? How will you get to work? What on earth will your boss say?"

Before I could get a word of answer in she finished the interrogation with, "You know you're a criminal now, right?"

Despite the grilling and being pumped with questions, I came out of the conversation relatively unscathed. In fact, bless her, she was very understanding. When I could finally get a word in to explain my plans, she seemed curiously interested in the concept of me riding to work given my age and fitness levels. She probably saw through my obvious attempt to play the whole thing down.

The new boss was also great when I told him that morning. He just looked at me impassively and, not knowing him very well, it was hard to read what he was thinking. I quickly offered to take leave, which I had plenty of, but being new he wasn't keen on that idea.

When I explained I could ride the e-bike into work, he looked at me, smiled and said, "No worries, we'll work in with you. I'd rather have you around."

I was genuinely relieved. I was going to keep my job, which was a big relief, but now I had opened my big mouth, twice! I was locked into riding to work. It was the first time—but certainly not the last over the next few months—that I realised I was completely and utterly mad.

Right, let's see if this can actually work. After talking the talk on how easy this would be, I now had to walk the walk, or ride the ride! How does a bloke in his 50s who hasn't ridden a bike any real distance since his teens traverse a forty-kilometre round trip on the rail trail which, incidentally, I'd never ridden on before and had no idea how long it would even take me! We Aries love nothing better than a challenge. I had no intention of letting this bit of adversity beat me. In hindsight, accepting this challenge was just as well!

After building what we thought was our "forever home" in Port Fairy, it became increasingly obvious that if I was ever going to be able to retire before they carried me off in a box, we would need to reduce our debt. We had a small mortgage, but it would still be a number of years before it was paid off. We also had literally all of our money tied up in the house, so we reluctantly decided to sell and buy something cheaper.

One of the unexpected results of COVID-19 (at least to me) was that the property market began to boom. People realised that COVID-19 was here to stay for a while, and with no overseas travel permitted, city folk began looking to rural areas. This trend was boosted by the rise of the home office and lockdowns restricting movement. Country areas became very much sought after as a location to live or holiday. So we sold our house, purchased a piece of land in Port Fairy and began the process of planning to build a house that would reduce our debt levels. We decided to move into rental accommodation in Koroit as there was nothing much available in Port Fairy at the time.

So to answer some of my burning logistical-travel-by-bike questions, I got up early the next weekend. The weather was fine, and with the promise of a sunny day, I packed some sunscreen and water and set off toward Warrnambool on the bike!

As I quietly stole along the streets of Koroit, I noticed most of the locals were still in bed. I began to consider the serendipity of moving to Koroit. If we had stayed in Port Fairy it would be impossible for me to ride to work every day because of the additional distance. I hoped Koroit was a manageable distance!

I purchased the e-bike for Jo for her birthday a few years previous. We called her Winona (later affectionately shortened to Winny), as it was a ladies e-bike after all. We purchased it with ambitious intent of trundling around Port Fairy, but we had hardly used it. It would definitely come in handy now! It has an electric motor which is essentially a pedal assist mechanism. When you push on the pedals, the motor kicks in, but the kicker is you actually have to pedal. I looked into buying one of those new pedal scooters which have a throttle, but I wasn't sure about the laws. I decided against it to avoid falling foul of the law and receiving a longer ban or going to prison where I was quite sure the food wouldn't agree with me. So it was going to be Winny and me from here on.

I planned to go just halfway on my first attempt. I needed to see if this was going to work and to test my untrained cycling legs. The rail trail is a very beautiful ride. The first section from Koroit takes you downhill around the edge of the Tower Hill ancient volcanic crater and is particularly scenic. The trail gently descends at a steady gradient through neatly kept farms with eucalypt-lined verges and all manner of farm animals and other wildlife who stared at me inquisitively as I passed. As I reached the bottom of the first section, my confidence was growing. Then, to my horror, I was staring at a small sign that said: "Warrnambool 13.4 km"! What? This was not even a quarter of the way! I was already knackered and I'd only been going downhill!

Oh well, on we go.

As I made my way from the bottom of the hill through the underpass under the Princes Highway and then onto the old Port Fairy Highway, I saw a thoughtfully fenced-off cycle path running beside the road. The road undulates and winds its way between farmland, horse paddocks and stables. The bike pulled me confidently up the rolling pathway, and I stopped at about the halfway point of my journey for a drink and to contemplate what I'd just done. My arms and shoulders were quietly aching, and my legs had decided they were no longer part of my body and that this was a stupid idea. I was tempted to call to be collected, but I clenched my fists, turned around and somehow accidentally swallowed a fly for good measure! Choking, I set off back up the hill toward home.

Remarkably, the return journey uphill was not as bad as I imagined. Riding Winny, which proper cyclists may think is cheating, got me back with about the same amount of effort as going downhill. This might just work! I reminded myself that this trip was only halfway to Warrnambool and not to get too ahead of myself. I rode home, parked the bike and flopped onto the sofa to recover. I'd answered a key question: at my pace, the ride would take about an hour each way. I could live with that.

The next morning, somewhat surprised at the lack of soreness, I readied myself for the full journey. Getting myself into my new sleek black bike shorts with elastised straps and Velcro strips that wrap around one's shoulders in a strange one-piece ensemble was something of a challenge. I balanced on one leg, jumping and flapping my arms around like a drunken contortionist and managed to don my newly-acquired riding attire for the mature gentleman. How on earth did the pros do this every day? The bloody straps bit into my shoulders, but I needed to look the part so I just went with it. I also invested in some "go fast" sunglasses with coloured lenses which made me look like a weird insect and a Darth Vader-style crash helmet to boot. Suitably attired, I set off on my newly-adopted mode of transport.

There are two alternative routes you can take to get from Koroit to Warrnambool: using the rail trail to avoid busy roads or taking those same busy roads. The roads are much more hectic with holidaymakers, caravans and all manner of boats and campervans eagerly trying to reach the beautiful southwest Victorian holiday spots in the summer. I planned to try one of these going out and one coming back to see which would suit me better.

The first option was to follow the rail trail all the way down Tower Hill, along the old Port Fairy road and through a series of wetlands and boardwalks that would eventually bring me out almost on the edge of the Warrnambool CBD. Ideal. The other likely option for a complete novice was to leave the rail trail on the outskirts of Warrnambool in Dennington, take a short section of the busy Princes Highway over the Merri River Bridge, then through the industrial estate into town. Fittingly, this was actually where I had been caught speeding to end up in this whole situation.

I decided to try the wetlands on the way there and the highway over the bridge on the way back so I could make a comparison. Nine o'clock on a Sunday morning probably wasn't representative of what I would encounter on a regular commute, as I would find out soon enough!

The trip down was uneventful, actually very pleasant. I made it in an hour, nothing bad happened and I felt pretty good considering I hadn't ridden this sort of distance since soon after Neil Armstrong and his chums Buzz Aldrin and Mike Collins landed on the moon.

I set off for the return leg that was not through the wetlands. I made steady progress until I came to a screeching halt at the Merri River Road bridge. The traffic! Trucks, busses, streams of cars, no real bike lane and only a skinny footpath on one side. As the COVID-19 pandemic dragged on and overseas travel was prohibited, there were considerably more holidaymakers flocking to the area for a local holiday destination. The roads were chockers!

As I wondered whether to risk life and limb crossing this apparent death trap, I watched as an older gentleman slowly and unwaveringly crossed the bridge without any hesitation. He was completely undeterred and went about his journey with an air of utter nonchalance. Inspired, I hopped back onto the bike, gripped the handlebars as if my life depended on it and rode as fast my legs would take me across the bridge. I was safely on the other side in about ten seconds. Sweet victory. There, that wasn't so bad, was it? Mmm, maybe I'd get used to it.

Reflecting on the experience after I got home, I felt relieved I was not due to hand in my driver's licence until January, so I still had a few sweet days until I surrendered my licence. This was proving vitally important planning time, as I realised I needed more practice to finally determine the best route. Physically I was OK and fairly confident I could manage the ride, but I was not entirely sure how I would hold up doing it five days in a row. The questionable safety of the bridge concerned me, but it was clearly a shorter route, and these burning questions bothered me somewhat.

So Monday morning, although still legally able to drive, I left the car at home and took the bike, I dispensed with the idea to wear the ridiculous bike shorts, which must have been designed by Harry Houdini as I found out trying to get out of them the day before, and dressed in my usual business attire. I did take the precaution of wearing a high visibility vest over my jacket to improve my chances of being seen.

As I left the house, the morning air was crisp and fresh, and despite being summer, my breath smoked in the early morning sunshine. The weather in these parts is varied and unpredictable at times. The temperature in summer is usually in the twenties Celsius, but it can get into the forties at times, which is usually pretty horrible. As we're near the coast we don't get many frosts, and the winters are wet and windy with temperatures usually around the low to mid-teens.

I recall one Christmas Day when some friends had travelled from England to visit me and have a hot Aussie Christmas. The temperature in Warrnambool and most of Victoria actually colder than it was in London! It even snowed in the mountains that year on Christmas Day, which was unheard of. On Boxing Day that year it was almost forty degrees and sweltering! So it was no surprise that mornings could be cool even during summer.

On the way I stopped to open some gates. This was a pain. These gates had always been open when I came through on the weekend, but the farmers must have blocked the rail trail for the cows to cross for milking. Some cows were walking slowly across my path. They looked friendly enough as I walked the bike along the trail amongst them. A large black and white cow stared disinterestedly at me, gave out a gentle low, and carried on past me as if this was an entirely normal thing to be doing. I had heard English farmers say "cush" to their cows to urge them along in movies, so I tried it, but these cows didn't react at all. Maybe it only worked in England. I made it through and shut the gates behind me to keep them in.

I had picked up a reasonable quantity of cow dung on my shoes, but I now turned my mind to the next hazard: the busy road bridge across the Merri River. I rode through the countryside on this fine cool morning; what a way to start the day. As I passed through the old railway embankment, the tall grass browned by the summer sun swooshed and swayed as I rattled and bumped down the deserted trail. The scene was stunning. Rolling pastures, tree-lined verges and the distant ocean formed a perfect backdrop. This wasn't so bad after all!

At the end of the cross-country section of the ride, I stopped and got off for a breather. From my vantage point, I had a good view of the road into Warrnambool. It was usually very busy with commuters, and this morning was no exception. There was a constant stream of cars and trucks all hurrying to get to work or wherever they were going. It had only taken about thirty minutes to reach the bridge. The traffic behind me had momentarily eased, so I set off across the bridge, but at the halfway point of the crossing three log trucks in convoy thundered past me. The wind they created was almost strong enough to blow me into the river, or worse, under their wheels. This was definitely not good. These logs trucks were huge. They each had three parts to them, one with the actual truck body full of logs and if that wasn't enough they had two trailers behind. They were road trains of logs! It vindicated my previous belief that this bridge was a bad idea and that riding across it was almost as stupid as losing my licence.

There had to be a better way. I really didn't want to start the day dreading the bridge crossing. Even though I was wearing a hi-vis ensemble, drivers around there can be pretty erratic, so I made a fateful decision. *That's it,* I thought, *it's through the wetlands both ways from now on.* That's when the fun really began.

2
Snakes Alive

To fully test the practicality of my commute solution, I decided to ride again the next day. The morning was overcast and there was a cold wind blowing from the north. This was supposed to be summer. Talk about global cooling!

After a freezing cold start to the ride, I entered the wetlands again. The wetlands are an eerie place at that time of the morning. They stretch for miles with what looks to be deep water, acres of tall reeds and hundreds of water birds. Just that morning I saw black swans, ibises and those curious birds which seem to run along the water as if it were boiling when taking off. In the afternoon on a sunny day it looks far more appealing, but on this cold, dismal morning it was deserted and almost creepy. It reminded me of a dreary place I visited in the Lake District in England named Wastwater, without the mountains. I was glad to pass through it and get onto the short road section which led to work.

Despite this, I reached the conclusion that, although longer and a bit creepy, I could safely avoid the perils of the Merri River Bridge on this route, so I would definitely go home this way. That took a worry off my mind. When driving to work, one doesn't have to worry about which way to travel home or the weather, so this was an entirely new experience for me.

When I reached work, I parked the bike in the bike shed.

"How was the ride this morning?"

It was my old mate Mick who had just arrived by car.

"Bloody freezing!" I said.

He smiled. "What time did you leave?"

"Quarter to seven from Koroit," I said casually.

"Nah, stuff that," he said and walked off smiling to himself

The cold morning warmed up into a lovely sunny and warm afternoon, perfect for my ride home. I packed my things into the saddlebags on the bike and set off for home in good spirits.

Shortly after entering the wetlands, I crossed a series of timber boardwalks that cross the water in places. I was cruising along at a comfortable speed of 30 km/h as I left the boardwalk and started on the path ahead when I saw a small snake. I can't tell you how much I don't like snakes—they terrify me. By the time I had seen it, I was going too fast to avoid it if it moved. Thankfully, it stayed basking in the late afternoon sunshine and seemed unfazed by my presence. As we live in the country, we are accustomed to the occasional encounter with a snake. They are few and far between, and usually brief—at least in my experience. I consciously avoided situations where I risked meeting a snake face to face. I put this encounter down as a one off, vowed to be more observant and carried on, eager to get home.

The trail takes you into some spectacularly beautiful natural wetlands named Kelly's Swamp, a name that doesn't lend credibility to the beauty of the place. Although I could see houses in the distance, it was quite a remote location away from civilisation. Tall rushes, clear water and vegetation border the trail. There is a long timber bridge that crosses the full width of the wetland which rattles and shakes as you cross it. Wild ducks, geese, water fowl, black swans and many other species of water birds flock to this rich, abundant area which I was admiring as I reflected on my working day. A group of pelicans swimming in convoy were feasting on fish and were not the least bit interested in anything else—and certainly not little old me on my lonesome.

It struck me that cyclists must be a solitary lot, well the ones that ride everywhere alone. For me riding alone in woop woop was ok, but in in small doses, akin to marzipan or tawny port. Riding home the trail narrowed in the distance. When I squinted into the late afternoon sunshine, I noticed a long, black, narrow shape draped across the entire width of the trail. My heart sank. I immediately knew immediately what it was. Snake! Big snake. Great, just great! I got off the bike and nervously scanned the area for any others that may be nearby. Nothing, phew! What were my options? I was miles from anywhere and faced with the prospect of having to turn back and cross the bridge. With the sun in my eyes, I couldn't tell what species it was, and I wasn't going to get closer to find out. In Australia most snakes are poisonous and must be treated with extreme caution, certainly from my point of view. I had heard there were snakes on the rail trail, but my eternal optimism said it wouldn't happen to me. Now I'd met two in one day.

I had visions of this angry reptile rearing up and becoming entangled in the spokes while biting me repeatedly! This was the stuff of nightmares. I stopped, got of the bike and started thinking about how I could get past this creature without needing an ambulance. I decided the best way was to scare it with something. I picked up a small stone and threw it with just enough force to land near it, hoping to scare it off the trail. The ruddy beast moved forward slightly but only a few paces (human paces—thank goodness snakes can't walk!), and it seemed stubbornly intent on enjoying the warmth of the trail and blocking my way home. Damn! I threw another stone, and this time it calmly and without haste took its time crossing the trail and slithered into the undergrowth.

Was it lurking beside the road lying in wait for this impertinent individual who had disturbed its afternoon repose? I didn't know. I got back on the bike and peddled as fast as I could past the area, hoping like hell that I would not be ambushed by a disgruntled serpent. Nothing. Big sigh of relief.

Hurrying through the remainder of the wetland, I anxiously and suspiciously checked any object in my path for fear of another chance encounter. I noticed how many sticks were on the trail, which from a distance could easily be a snake cunningly disguised. My heart raced from the anxiety and the ride.

On reflection, there was probably nothing to worry about as snakes are generally only interested in food, water and self-preservation, but I wasn't taking any chances. Two snakes in one afternoon were quite enough, thank you. It occurred to me that, much like sharks, these surrounds are snakes' natural habitat. If it wasn't such a naturally beautiful area with the water and the birds, frogs and other lovely creatures, the snakes would probably not be there but neither would the other creatures. It was a wetland, and there are snakes in Australian wetlands.

If you are frightened of snakes like me, don't miss out on riding the rail trail. Maybe don't go through the wetlands on a hot day during the summer months. So far, I hadn't seen a snake anywhere else on the trail, and it's a beautiful ride.

The remainder of the trip home was without incident and snake-less, but I was on edge. I might have to reconsider this route. It wasn't exactly the relaxing ride home at the end of a long day I had envisaged.

The next day was the last day I was allowed to drive, so it began with me packing the bike into the back of the car. I would drive to work and then ride home that night. I surrendered my licence at the VicRoads office, gave the company car to a colleague and accepted that I was going to be on two wheels instead of four for the next three months.

As an incurable optimist, I decided to go through the wetlands on my way home despite the previous day's snake encounter. Maybe it was just bad luck, a one off. Did I mention I'm an incurable optimist?! After feverishly pedalling most of the way through the wetlands and thinking maybe this route was fine after all, sure enough I saw the long, slithering Joe Blake ahead getting a tan on the warm path. The third snake in two days!

Maybe that bridge wasn't too bad after all. The question was: How would I prefer to die? The slow death of a snake bite in the middle of nowhere or the relative appeal of a sudden "death by log truck"? Easy choice. I'd take the log trucks any day of the week even with two trailers. At least I could finish up in the river, which might be a pleasant way to die on a warm afternoon. Upon reaching this conclusion, I relived the whole speeding incident on repeat and went over the things I might have said to persuade the police officers to just fine me and not take my licence away. There was no realistic chance of changing the outcome of the speeding saga, so I resolved to pull myself together, stop acting like a rabbit in the headlights and get on with my commute.

Rest was hard to come by that night. In my dreams, sticks turned into e-bike eating snakes, and a demented holidaymaker in a hotted up, high speed motor home was bent on squishing me like a bug on his windscreen. Not exactly a peaceful sleep.

I hatched a cunning plan in the cold light of the next day. There are traffic lights at the supermarket before the bridge which should, in theory, hold up the traffic long enough for me to scarper over the bridge safely. And on the way back there is the footpath on the far side. By waiting for a break in the traffic, I might actually get across without soiling my work clothes, causing an accident or both. Why hadn't I thought of this before! I rode to the outskirts of Warrnambool, stopped at the bridge, hopped off the bike and waited for the traffic to clear. And waited. Kept waiting. Still waiting—where are all these people going?!

Then there was a break in the traffic—go, go, go! I made it; the plan worked.

Going home that night was the same predicament. It was OK to wait for the traffic. I imagined the hard-core road riders and city cyclists in fits of laughter at this, but hey....

I had the route sussed by the end of the first week. There and back, up and down at 25 km/h with no stopping or turning back. Things went along OK for a while... until the cows intervened.

3

A Short Cut To A Stampede

I've always quite liked cows. I've mainly admired them from a safe distance, vicariously, without getting to know their individual personalities, and I confess I'm partial to the odd Sunday lunch of roast beef.

As I rode home on my second week on the bike, I became slightly more adventurous and decided to take what I thought might be a short cut. Leaving my usual route, I crossed the road to see if a gravel road joining the rail trail farther up might save me some time. I noticed a farmer in the distance opening a gate to let his cows cross a gravel road, so I waited thinking they would calmly pass ahead of me.

Maybe they disliked my red hi-vis vest or they were in a foul mood, but they stopped, looked directly at me and collectively bolted straight toward me. To make things worse, one of these beasts was what the Scots call a "hippy cow"—a massive, shaggy animal with long horns. This one looked as though his had been honed to a point by painstakingly sharpening them on a mangled e-bike from a previous encounter. If that thing got hold of me I'd have pennies on my eyes in no time. Gored to death on an e-bike by a hippy cow is not something I would be proud of on my tombstone.

The farmer was on a quad bike and began wildly waving his arms and shouting something inaudible but likely along the lines of "Get the hell out of the way!" With around forty seemingly pissed off bovines bearing down on me at full speed (led by the Scottish hippy cow), I decided whatever he was shouting was probably right. I took off at full bore back the way I had come. What I hadn't factored in was that the farmer was taking the cows the full length of the road I had just come down to get to another paddock near the end of the road. I ventured a look over my left shoulder and saw that the cows were making a good fist of keeping up with me, so I pedalled as fast as my still relatively untrained legs would take me.

At this point I should mention that e-bikes have a curious feature; well, ours does anyway. Sometimes the electric motor does not kick in straight away. Damn, Winny where are you? C'mon! Where's the motor? I was in full flight but completely under my own steam, which is why the motor wasn't engaged. Once you reach the speed restricted on the bike in order to make it legal in Victoria, the pedal assist cuts out. It's only when you slow down that it kicks in, like when going up a hill, but this road was dead flat, and I wasn't slowing down for anything, motor or not.

By this time the farmer had caught up with me on his quad bike. He was wildly gesticulating for me to keep going while he continued to yell something unintelligible. I concluded that they didn't actually speak English in this part of Warrnambool, but I got the gist of what he wanted me to do. These cows were unlike anything I'd ever seen or experienced before. Usually docile, slightly inquisitive animals, I had never really seen them as predatory.

I estimated the road was about one kilometre, and I hoped I had enough pedal power to outsprint them to safety. I don't suppose anybody got to witness this, but it must have looked quite a sight. A red-vested geezer hammering along a gravel road on an e-bike with about thirty tons of prime beef in hot pursuit. At this point I thought I might suggest that the manufacturers of e-bikes provide optional extras such as a warp speed setting and a death ray for emergency situations such as these. Behind me the girls were bellowing and roaring in apparent frustration at the fact that I was getting away.

After what seemed like hours, I finally saw the end of the road and the rail trail and safety. I could also see that the only gate that could possibly be the cow's destination was open and partially blocking the road. The farmer on his pesky quad bike must have opened it after I came through. As if it wasn't bad enough being chased by what seemed to be much of the OK Corral, I had to skilfully navigate a small gap between the gate and the remainder of the road. Skill and agility was not actually something I had acquired as yet. I may have closed my eyes for an instant as I shot through the gap because I don't remember how close I came to crashing into it. I somehow managed to get through the opening without taking off my knee caps or—even worse—crashing headlong into the gate.

I rode another few hundred metres and paused to ensure the cows were safely herded into the new paddock. I waited until the gate was locked. The hippy cow bellowed one last time in my general direction as if demanding a rematch. The farmer also decided to have one final word on the matter. He flapped his arms and shouted something in his native tongue which, I could tell by his mannerisms, was not entirely complimentary. I accepted my admonishment and turned for home, still shaken. I decided that short cuts were on the list of stupid things I had done in my life along with losing my licence.

As I rode home up Tower Hill, a magnificent wedge-tailed eagle perched on a fence post stared placidly at me. This reminded me that this really was a beautiful part of the world and I was lucky to have this experience in nature. It sat there without any fear of me and allowed me to take its picture on my phone.

I thanked Winny for getting me home when we arrived.

"Next time, if you don't mind awfully, give me a hand when a posse of cows has a go at us!"

I hung the helmet on the handlebars. That was close! As I entered the house, Jo asked how the ride was.

"Oh, not too bad really," I said casually, playing it down so she wouldn't worry. "Had a bit of trouble with some cows on the road, but we were too quick for 'em."

Memories typically fade in time, and I had already begun to see the funny side of my encounter. In bed that night I imagined the perils of attacking cows that had been somehow trained to run at an unnatural pace to see off any would-be intruders. I firmly decided I would not stray from the path in the future.

4

The Railway and a Cheeky Wallaby

Keen to keep my fitness up, I decided to ride from Koroit to Port Fairy on the Australia Day public holiday in January 2021. The weather was much cooler than the previous few days, so it was a perfect time to explore this part of the trail. It spans about nineteen kilometres, virtually the same distance as the Koroit to Warrnambool section.

I started at the old Koroit railway station, which is a must see. The station buildings are very well kept and take you right back in time to the early part of the twentieth century when they were built. The main station house is built of red brick under a red clay tiled roof with two rows of contrasting cream rendered bricks at intervals that bisect the walls and an elaborate cantilevered veranda overhanging the old platform. There is railway paraphernalia still in place such as the levers to pull the tracks from one side to another. The flashing red lights have been wired to be flashing constantly, which is a nice touch especially as there would be no trains coming these days.

The last train to this station was in September 1977, and I remember catching the train from Warrnambool to Port Fairy as a young guy. I imagine it must have been in the 1970s not long before the whole thing was wrapped up. There is a great children's playground at the old station now, which would be a nice diversion from the trail for families with children. The old goods shed is pretty well intact.

The trail is asphalt for a stretch leaving Koroit, which is nice underfoot or under pedal. I splashed along through puddles left behind from some welcome overnight rain. From there it passes through a tree-lined section where I encountered a flock of yellow-tailed black cockatoos who cawed at me as I rode past. I've always liked these birds whenever I saw them. They seem to sound far away even if they are quite close, and they kept up their chorus as they flew off into distant pine trees. Unlike the more common sulphur-crested cockatoos which are white and have a really noisy screech, the black ones have a gentle, more melodic cry.

A small bush wallaby was grazing up ahead, and it bounded off as I approached. It was probably used to seeing people and bikes on the rail trail so didn't seem startled, more like it was just going about its business farther up the trail. As I got nearer, it stopped and turned around almost checking to see if I was keeping up. It had plenty of opportunity to hop off the trail and out of my path but continued to bound ahead for a few hundred metres or so. Then it stopped and waited for me again. It reminded me of a sheep dog I once used to race in my car. It would lie in wait behind its front fence on my approach, then excitedly race the full length of its front garden trying to outpace me. Reaching the end of the garden it would bark delightedly as I drove off into the distance. And sure enough this little wallaby seemed to be doing the same thing—bound off, wait and so on. This went on for about five minutes until it eventually left the trail and headed off to the side into a stand of gum trees. Would I see it on the way back?

The Koroit to Port Fairy ride is quite different from the Warrnambool section. The route took me entirely on the old rail corridor, unlike much of the Warrnambool segment which follows the road for a good part and then through the wetlands. As I rode merrily along into a stiff headwind, quite a few other riders and walkers politely greeted me as I passed. Unlike the part of Warrnambool where I encountered the cows, these folk all spoke English. As it was a public holiday there were noticeably more people on the trail. There were never many daily commuters, if any at all most days.

The trail is long and flat to Port Fairy with wide sections of the trail corridor and long, straight stretches. Passing over small bridges and creeks, you eventually catch sea glimpses in the distance as you approach the settlement. There are more trees through parts of the journey which break up the scenery and provide somewhere to enjoy the shade or to shelter if it rains.

On my approach to Port Fairy, I could see lines of traffic and caravans as visitors were heading home after their summer holidays. As I crossed the roadway, a car inexplicably started hooting its horn at me. I wondered if it was the cow farmer who recognised me, but then thought it was more likely to be somebody I knew that was laughing at the hilarity of seeing me on a bike.

I seriously considered putting one of those red safety flags on the bike, but then thought it might be better to avoid drawing too much attention to myself in case there was another cow experience. Besides, it would slow me down and give the wallaby an unfair advantage.

I'd lived in Port Fairy for a number of years, so I decided not to venture into the village happy in the thought that it was an achievable ride should I decide to head that way again.

The tiny hamlets of Crossley and Kirkstall are signposted remnants from the railway days where I imagined the train drivers of a bygone era would toot the whistle as they passed by. What other purpose could the signs be for? There were no stations at these places, simply signs. It's not as if the train driver could get lost without them in a perfectly straight line with only one route on rails available. Maybe trains used to stop at these places to let people off and on? I liked the signs and their history, and I stopped to take pictures of each one. I later read that the signs were situated at railway sidings where farm produce was loaded to be sent off to various markets and other destinations to be sold. The area is well known for its produce, particularly potatoes. If you haven't been to Warrnambool or Port Fairy you really should visit.

My focus was on getting back to Koroit to enjoy Australia Day. *Doing the rail trail on an e-bike is probably cheating*, I thought as I effortlessly passed grimacing riders on the uphill parts of the ride. I'm sure some of them were looking at me enviously, muttering "Bastard!" under their breath. I've probably helped sell a few e-bikes as a consequence of my escapade.

The wallaby was nowhere in sight on the return journey; perhaps it was off celebrating the famous victory when it easily outpaced an e-bike.

Arriving back in Koroit, some of the rail trail volunteers were doing some gardening at the old station. It occurred to me that I must have been getting fitter, as I was usually focused on getting home alive without being attacked by something, having a seizure or winding up in the river. I noticed how much work it must be to keep the trail in good condition, and I thought about the hours and hours it must take to keep it well maintained and beautiful. And it really is.

As I pedalled past the old station, I noticed the doors were open and there were folks sitting inside and outside the building having a cup of tea or coffee. I found out later that it was a fundraising day as the rail trail is largely maintained by volunteers, although the local councils do provide some maintenance. It's a big job and a credit to everyone involved.

5

The Wild Southwest

Southwest Victoria is a beautiful and varied place. It takes in The Great Ocean Road, the Grampians (a range of mountains and a national park) and some of the most stunning coastlines and beaches I have seen anywhere in the world. It tends to be cooler than other parts of Australia and rains more, which makes it lush for much of the year. There are rainforests, rivers and wetlands with wide expanses of pasture providing a thriving agricultural and fishing industry.

It had been two weeks since I had given back my car and stopped driving. Living with Jo helped, of course, because she took care of the essentials. I didn't fancy the thought of riding home with a twenty-kilogram bag of dry dog food for our three Labradors balanced precariously across my shoulder. But it was no trouble to ride down the hill into Koroit to grab a coffee or the paper on the weekend. The little town had pretty much all we needed on a day-to-day basis, and I could easily get there on the bike.

If you haven't been to Koroit it's also well worth a visit. It gets somewhat overshadowed by the coastal towns of Warrnambool and Port Fairy, but it certainly has plenty of charm and appeal. There are some superb old buildings and really well-maintained weatherboard or brick Victorian-era homes. The centre of town is filled with quaint Victorian shops which still have most of their original architectural features such as ornate verandas and some original signage. There is even the odd horse trough depicting the horse-drawn days. It is a bit like stepping back in time. The townsfolk take pride in their town, and I frequently saw locals walking around picking up litter out of pride in the village or out of sheer boredom, or both. Their gardens are really beautiful. Lovely deciduous trees—mostly oaks and elms—mix with some of the best roses I have seen anywhere. Despite being very much Australian, Koroit has a European feel to it with some very pretty little churches. The locals are also very friendly and welcoming, usually smiling or saying hello or simply raising one finger (not the middle one) in a typical one-fingered Aussie greeting as they pass you by in a car.

One aspect of this part of the country which is of particular appeal to me is stargazing. The skies are very clear at times with the absence of street lighting in rural areas. The stars are spectacularly clear and bright. One morning as I was getting ready to leave for work it was not quite light and I noticed a curious phenomenon in the sky. A row of what looked like about twenty stars were moving slowly in a dead straight line before disappearing one by one behind a cloud. Puzzled at what I was watching, I wondered if I had just seen my first UFO encounter. It certainly was odd! That night when I recounted my sighting to Jo, we took to the internet for any clues as to what this strange sight might have been. And there staring back at me was the very image of what I had seen. It turned out that the entrepreneur Elon Musk had launched a heap of satellites to beam high speed internet services. I was amazed but also a little disappointed that the mystery had a scientific explanation and not some evocative alien craft encounter.

Of a more terrestrial nature, Koroit got its name, Koroitch Gundidj, from the Indigenous Australians who lived in the area. It has been abbreviated to Koroit today. The first European settlers came to Koroit in 1837, and it was particularly popular with the Irish people who came to Australia at that time. Port Fairy was originally named Belfast. Names like O'Sullivan, Quinlan, Keane and O'Brien are prevalent, and the presbytery building next to the church could easily be in the set of an Irish film. In fact, I posted some photos of some of the buildings online without saying where they were. Some comments asked, "Where are you mystery man?"

There is a rich indigenous history of the area which is ancient, fascinating and confronting. It is not for me to tell this story, but if you have a passion for local history I encourage you to visit the various websites on the subject. A great one to look at is Moyjil Warrnambool, but there are many others.

These days the people of Koroit must surely hold the world record for the number of ride-on mowers per capita. Everyone seems to own one! It's probably because, unlike much of the urban landscape of Australia which is being cut into small pieces of land for higher density living, this is most definitely not the case in Koroit. Lot sizes in Australia are getting smaller and smaller in cities and towns as the ever-increasing demand for urban housing continues. It's not necessarily a bad thing as it can be a smart use of infrastructure. However, on weekend afternoons in Koroit you will hear a full orchestral symphony of residents on their ride-ons. The volcanic soil in Koroit is perfect for growing all manner of things, and homeowners generally have big gardens with wide expanses of lawns, hence the mowers.

There is one curious thing I'd not figured out as yet. Some people leave their garage doors open when they are home. If it's a double garage, only one door is wide open. I had never encountered this strange phenomenon before. Was it ventilation, habit or a peace offering to the volcano Gods of Tower Hill to minimise the risk of another eruption? I made a mental note to ask around and get to the bottom of this weird garage door business. Tower Hill is a dormant (not extinct) volcano which provides a stunning landmark almost equidistant between Warrnambool and Port Fairy. It is believed to have last erupted about thirty-two thousand years ago. The volcano formation is known today as nested maar. As indigenous Australians are known to have been in the area at the time, remarkably some may have actually witnessed eruptions at Tower Hill. When I went to school in Warrnambool in the 1970s, my science teachers called it a nested caldera. Essentially, the volcano blew its brains out and left a massive crater where the mountain had once been. If you know this part of southwest Victoria, you will know that much of the basalt between Port Fairy and Koroit came from explosions at Tower Hill, including the basalt all the way on the coastline.

Tower Hill became Victoria's first national park in 1892. It is home to a wide variety of native wildlife including kangaroos, wallabies, emus, koalas and many species of birds and other wildlife. There are, of course, snakes, so keep your eyes open if you go bushwalking. Sadly, Tower Hill was deforested many years ago, so the government undertook tree planting in the 1970s in an effort to restore its natural beauty. School children like me did much of the planting. I vividly remember a school bus full of rowdy kids getting dropped off at Tower Hill to hunker down in the rain halfway up the crater walls to plant trees. I wasn't much good at it, and most of my trees probably died, but it was fun to take part. School kids have planted thousands of native trees over the years, and today it is pretty well-forested in many sections as a result (probably with no help from me). Informative and fun guided tours take visitors to various parts of the reserve, and the guides know the best places to see the various types of wildlife.

Warrnambool is the largest town on the rail trail. Situated at the end of the Great Ocean Road, it lies some 260 km west of Melbourne. It has an array of period buildings dating back to Victorian times which border dunes and long sandy beaches. It's edged by two rivers leading into the sea—the Hopkins and the Merri—and is well known for its milk and dairy production. Warrnambool is particularly famous for whale watching from May to September when the southern right whales come to the waters to calve. There is a strong sporting culture covering most sports, excellent dining and shopping and a regional hospital. Warrnambool plays an important role in providing employment, tourism and essential services to the region.

I grew up in Warrnambool before living in lots of places, including the UK for 15 years. My most vivid memory of Koroit was playing Aussie Rules Football (a game closer to rugby than soccer) against them. I played for South Warrnambool like my father did, but he was better than I was. He played for North Melbourne which is, for those of you who don't know, the best team in the universe and very generous allowing most teams to beat them these days out of the goodness of their hearts. He came to live in Warrnambool and played for South Warrnambool who are the second best in the universe. I played in the area from the age of twelve until I left at twenty years old. I went on to play in Bendigo for South Bendigo and also for St Albans in Melbourne. I probably wasn't big enough to make a profession out of it, but I played some reasonably good games of country footy, unlike Dad who played in the big league.

I can't remember winning a game against Koroit. When we played Koroit in Koroit we were invariably flogged. It may have something to do with their size! The Koroit boys were big—really big. This was probably due to the fact that most of the kids were farmers' boys, raised on hard labour. The area is renowned for its potato and dairy farms, and before school or after a bruising game of football, they would go back to milk the cows or pick spuds. What hope did we have? The Warrnambool city folk had probably never milked a cow or picked a spud—I certainly never had—and our soft, cushy, coastal lifestyle was no match for these hardened individuals. They were never dirty players, but boy were they big and tough. I remember watching them run onto the field before us when I was playing junior footy. *Geez they're big.*

As you can probably imagine, given the vastness of Australia and the distances between places, living without a car, especially in the country, is about as funny as a broken leg. Getting around entirely by bike or on foot was a new experience, but somehow I got the hang of it fairly quickly. I didn't have the luxury of popping home when I forgot something, so I found myself meticulously checking that I had everything before setting off. Forgetting house keys, wallet or a mask (because of the wretched pandemic) could be catastrophic and mean a long ride back which was not really possible due to how long it would take or doing without it for the whole day. We had also equipped the bike with a puncture kit, bike pump and a handy drink holder for coffee or a water bottle. The bike didn't have the comforts of a car, but so far it did the job.

Luckily, I was still able to do the occasional day working from home due to the pandemic restrictions. This came in handy on really wet days or even this week when forty degrees was forecast, followed by rain later. I was able to work from home on occasions so didn't always have to brave the elements.

If you are going to lose your driver's licence, living not too far from work and being able to work from home a bit makes it easier. I've always been something of a fatalist, and despite believing in karma I realised I was dealing with this penance quite well so far. As it turned out, I was just at the beginning of the story.

It was back to work and the rail trail after the long weekend. Riding to work that Tuesday, I felt I had settled into something of a routine, which was a comfort I needed. Now that I am older, I actually don't like being out of my comfort zone. It may stem from a fear of the unknown which is strange when I look back I was always an adventurist as a child, and certainly as a teenager. When I was 16 years old I was amongst the first few exchange students from Australia to spend a year in the USA. As a fresh faced country boy I had the privilege to spend a year in Indiana with a wonderful family who spoiled me rotten. They took me to many parts of the country as I spent my Junior year running track and field, playing tennis for my school and getting up to all sorts. I even had a walk on part in the school play which enabled the organisers to say that *"this years' play has an international cast"*. My family and friends back home naturally mocked the American accent I had acquired living there. I made many American friends who are in touch with me to this day including my old doubles partner and of course my host family whom I regularly contact via social media. The trip certainly put me in good stead for adulthood. As a child I was fearless and inquisitive. I once tied my mother's apron to my back and jumped off the garage roof to see if it worked as a parachute. Of course, it failed miserably and I sprained my ankle, but I got into less trouble than the time I decided to see if my mother's Mozart collection of 78 records would fly like a Frisbee. That was the first and only time I ever heard my mother use the "F" word. As I have aged, I am less of a risk taker and certainly less destructive.

The predictability of what lay ahead on the journey was somehow comforting. It must have something to do with getting older. My life had been tipped upside down so even sights and smells riding to work were familiar and gave me time to think and reminisce. Because I didn't have to concentrate on the traffic and what was going on around me when driving, I actually had time to muse and reflect on life, which I didn't expect; it was quite pleasant.

I was thinking about karma for some reason that day. I created plenty of mischief and havoc growing up, and perhaps this whole situation was some sort of pay back for those times. Whenever my sister Mandy and I played Monopoly, she had to be the dog token, and she won every time! So I smashed it with a hammer. It was important to destroy weapons of power in the family. She did, however, get me back one day. I had ordered a Skippy the Kangaroo plate from a coupon on the back of a breakfast cereal packet. The plate was advertised as "unbreakable," which particularly appealed to me. I was something of a klutz and always getting into trouble for breaking things. After months of waiting, it finally arrived.

"Unbreakable? Let's see," Mandy said.

She took it out into the backyard, raised it above her head and threw it as hard as she could on the concrete path, smashing it to pieces. I was so convinced it was unbreakable, I cried my eyes out when the unthinkable happened. Being the mischievous little brother that I was, I deserved it. Sibling rivalry was alive and well in our household. My long-awaited Skippy plate was in a thousand pieces on the back lawn.

Of course, there were downsides to riding the bike to work. Getting a dragonfly caught in my helmet and being smacked in the face by insects and swallowing flies were unintended consequences. However, at least I hadn't fallen off the bike, been gored to death by a Scottish hippy cow or drowned. I was grateful to live in Australia, as I would definitely not like to lose my licence in Africa or Russia and have to contend with a lion, cheetah or a bear. I wouldn't have a hope even on a Russian version of Winny (or Winovska?) and would probably freeze to death in a Siberian winter.

A minor challenge was getting through the various stock crossings that cross the trail on my way to work, especially in the wetland section. I discovered that the one nearest home was always open before 7:00 a.m., but usually closed after that to allow the cows to cross the trail to be milked. I made it my business to get through this section before seven in the morning (peak cow rush hour) to avoid having to open the gates, walk through the lines of cows and shut the gates afterwards. Unlike the Dennington version, these were friendly cows, but I tried to avoid any delays.

I also found that people I really needed to speak to would ring at the most inconvenient time on my ride. Really? You've had all day to call me back, but you choose the moment I'm slogging into a hot headwind, uphill with my shoe laces undone?! Wow.

Having said that, my friends at work were really considerate and often offered rides. I was genuinely touched by their generosity. Two weeks into my driving ban, I hadn't had to prevail on anyone, but I expected that there would be times I would.

Our three Labradors found my new mode of transport particularly intriguing. I was initially greeted at the front gate in my bike helmet and sunglasses with furious barking. Having owned dogs for many years, particularly Labradors, I can read their expressive faces and mannerisms, so it is quite easy to know what they would be saying if they could speak.

"Go away you weird thing! This is our house! Don't get any closer…"

As I took off my helmet and sunglasses, they realised who I was and began to smile and wag their tails. I'd open the garage let them in and put the bike on charge and could see they were interested.

"Dad, where on earth have you been all day? Where's the car? Your legs smell funny."

They took a keen interest in sniffing the bike.

"Mmm, essence of cow dung, a bit of perspiration. What's this red dirt? You know, Dad, you can be really weird sometimes. Can we play with the ball? What time is dinner?"

After the first couple of weeks they got the hang of it, and by the end of January they had worked out what time I would arrive home and began to wait for me at the gate to greet me. Most dogs are great, unlike a few of the characters that I would encounter riding around.

6

When It Rains, It Pours

It was a Friday of my second week riding the bike to work. The forecast was for rain and strong winds. I had received offers of a lift to work the night before from sympathetic colleagues concerned about me riding in the bad weather and also from Jo, but I was on a quest. I needed to experience a sudden rainstorm or showers to know if I could hack it.

The rain was steadily falling, and when I said goodbye to Jo at 6:45 a.m. to beat the peak cow rush hour traffic, she said, "You're not going out in that?!"

"Yes, they're only showers," I scoffed.

"You're crazy!" she said.

The response was not entirely unexpected. I have been described as a man of contradictions, which is a probably a nice way of saying I am a bit crazy.

I set off hoping the rain was a passing shower, but it was actually the kind of rain that soaks you to the skin. Even before reaching the rail trail I was very wet. My "waterproof" hi-vis jacket was anything but. The rain had penetrated through it driven by a strong headwind, so my work clothes were wringing wet, socks and shoes soaked and my face was getting stung by heavy rain drops as I pushed headlong into the torrent.

I made it through the cow crossing before the gates were closed across the trail. Good! However, I'd only travelled about two kilometres, so I was resigned to the fact that I would get very wet riding to work. I had prepared for this day by leaving a change of clothes at the office, so at least I would be dry in about an hour. Sloshing along, I was trying to remember if I had left a spare pair of shoes at work.

After about thirty minutes I reached the Merri River Bridge. The rain was finally easing, but the damage was done. I was a drowned rat. Crossing the bridge shouldn't have been particularly cold, but the strong headwind chilled my wet body to the bone.

The summer had been anything but. The weather had been warm some days, but it was a "La Niña" year. Apparently this weather system was named by some Spanish fisherman bloke, and it meant "Little Girl." I couldn't help thinking that this weather was anything but little and nothing like what a girl should resemble. If anything, it was more akin to a big girl bully that would belt you in the school playground!

Anyway, it was my own fault. I had chosen to endure this so there was no point complaining.

There was a small crowd of onlookers at work who must have anticipated my arrival given the inclement weather. My e-bike adventures seemed to be the talk of the office, so they were not disappointed when I sloshed in that day. My clothing hung limply off my body, my face was mud-splattered, and when I stopped at the back door they stared at me in total disbelief.

"I can't believe you rode in that!" said Peter.

"Oh that's nothing," I said casually. "Just a bit damp this morning."

Of course, this was complete nonsense, but I eagerly grabbed my bag of dry clothes and rushed into the men's toilets to get changed, leaving wet footprints on the carpet as I went. I immediately checked the bag of clothes for shoes. Nothing! Damn and blast. I immediately felt a lot better when I changed into my dry wardrobe, but I had to figure my shoe situation. I would have to buy new ones. I couldn't stand having wet feet all day, and walking around in bare feet was not the professional demeanour I was trying to exude. I was already the centre of my co-workers' amusement, so I didn't want to draw extra attention. There was also a farewell lunch that day for a colleague at a restaurant where I was quietly confident I would not be admitted in bare feet.

There was nothing else for it, I would have to improvise. The shops weren't open until 9:30 a.m. and it was only eight o'clock, so I squelched my way around the office, leaving little puddles wherever I had been. I was also chilled from spending an hour in sopping wet clothes and a voracious headwind.

At 9:30, I squished all the way up the street to the show shop. I left a trail of water to the men's shoe section, and the shop girl stared at my feet suspiciously as I browsed. It didn't take Sherlock Holmes to solve the mystery of who left the footprints on the floor she had recently cleaned. I decided to buy two pairs of shoes so I could leave one at work if I got caught out again in a deluge.

"Ah yes, these are a good choice, Sir. They are puddle resistant," she said with a smile.

If she wondered why my feet were soaked and my clothes dry, she didn't ask. She must think me a little too old to be wantonly jumping into puddles for the sheer insane humour of it.

Aahh, that was better. With dry feet, I could now concentrate on something other than the chill in my lower extremities and not be the centre of attention at the farewell lunch.

As the day wore on, my energy flagged. I had already ridden two hundred kilometres that week and had likely used up more energy trying to stay warm during the ride in the rain. I also lugged around the dozens of kilograms of wet clothes from my saturated body riding in. As it was forecast to rain most of the day, I decided to be a bit sensible and to ask one of my colleagues for a lift part of the way home with the bike in the back. I could ride the remainder of the way to have a nice quiet end to the week as far as riding went. Jo and I were also invited to my brother and sister-in-law's house for dinner that night, so a ride would give me time to freshen up.

I gratefully packed the bike into my colleague's van, and we set off for home. Very civilised I thought as we drove along. Two weeks of my ban done and dusted and I'd be home in a jiffy. It's funny how things don't always turn out as you expect.

Being dropped off at the underpass under the highway left me an easy six-kilometre ride home with plenty of time to spare. I got onto the bike and set off in high spirits. A short time later suddenly the bike seat cracked and slipped. Whoa! What just happened? As I got off the bike, the seat got off with me—well, it fell off, really. The bolt holding it to the seat shaft had sheared clean off and bits of it were missing. Did they fall off on the trail? There was no way of reattaching it!

I tried standing up on the pedals, but the bike is quite heavy and it was really hard work. I stopped to ponder the situation. The sky was darkening and threatening more rain. Having already experienced a biblical style flood that morning, I put my improvisational skills to the test again.

Maybe if I sat on the plastic bag full of wet shoes and clothes as a makeshift seat I could bear riding home? When I tried this, all the wet clothes fell out behind me as I rode off, including the new trousers I had been given as a Christmas present only a few weeks before. Losing them would not be the smartest move, so I needed a better solution. I took the clothes out of the bag and wrapped them over the seat shaft, which meant I was able to sit with only severe rather than excruciating discomfort. As I got going, they slipped backwards onto the bike rack holding the saddlebags and me with it. Actually, this was OK. Although leaning backward at a bizarre angle was kind of odd, at least I could reach the pedals and control the bike in a weirdly reclined position.

I made slow but steady progress as I approached the cow crossing, which was now a quagmire of mud and other odorous material. I had less control of the bike from my unusual angle and prayed I could keep from skidding off into what looked and smelled like the residue of a septic tank. Amazingly, my makeshift bike seat held. As the damp clothes soaked into my trousers, wetness gradually enveloped my bottom. It was gratifying that I had successfully negotiated the cow crossing hazard, the reverse of which would have neatly topped off a difficult day.

I reached home at last and, thankfully, smelled pretty normal. I showed Jo the damaged seat, and she was amused at the thought of how ridiculous I must have looked sitting on the bike rack with my wet clothes for cushioning. After I changed clothes, we took the seat shaft out, put the broken seat in the car and headed for dinner at my brother and sister-in-law's place. My brother Tim is an avid cyclist and has some serious road and other two-wheeled pedal varieties, not to mention a garage full of parts and accessories and the skill to effect the repair to the seat.

As he was fixing Winny, he laughed when I told him the story of the seat falling off and how I managed to make it home sitting on the bike rack.

"Do you think you might keep riding for fun when you are back driving?" he asked, always keen to encourage more bikers.

"Yeah, I think so" I said.

"Well, you might like to keep a spare seat and the parts in the bag. Here, let me show you how to put a seat on if it comes off again," he said dryly.

"Cheeky sod," I said.

Grateful that the bike was back on the road and that I could ride in a more sober position, I thanked him and we drove home. I didn't fancy the indignity of sitting on the bike rack to collect the Saturday morning coffee in front of the locals. I was also keen to use the bike over the weekend to keep my eye in and my fitness up.

Yes, this certainly was a day of improvisation.

7

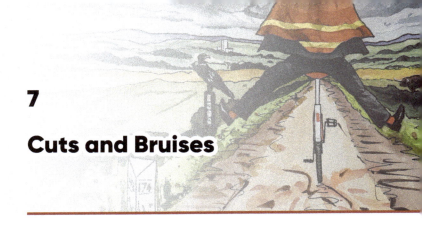

Cuts and Bruises

The likelihood of crashing the bike was inevitable. It was just a matter of when (not if) and how badly. Well, I didn't have to wait long to find out as I began my third week of riding.

The ride into Warrnambool was uneventful; it was becoming routine. With the office within sight, I was focused on the day ahead and not on crossing a railway siding. When the front tyre of the bike caught the edge of the rail, the bike slipped effortlessly out from under me and *whoomp!* It sounded like a small building being demolished as I hit the ground. I was unceremoniously dumped on the roadside with a grunt. I wasn't immediately concerned with how bad any injuries may be because I wanted to reassure concerned passers-by that it was a minor incident.

"Nothing to see here, just a flesh wound. Thanks very much."

The interesting thing about pain is that it has a tendency to sneak up on you. I was shaken but, surveying various abrasions, the prognosis was generally OK. I gathered up a variety of flotsam and jetsam that had flown from the saddlebags—spilt water, sunglasses, fractured muesli bars—and got back on with a degree of suspicion. I gingerly rode the short distance to the office.

I slunk into the office and headed straight toward the toilet hoping my colleagues wouldn't catch a look at my situation.

"Hey what are those cuts all over you?"

Busted. It was Steve, a very experienced rider. Of all the people, just my luck! Damn, my humiliation had begun.

"Oh, I came off the bike just now, nothing serious," I ventured in a casual tone.

"You OK?"

"Yeah, fine thanks."

"Yeah it's good for ya falling off," he said as I crept into the cubicle, locked the door and slumped onto the toilet to rest.

He was trying to put my mind at ease and genuinely meant well, but I could think of many things that were good for me—relaxing in a spa, a decent night's sleep or swimming with dolphins came to mind. But crashing heavily to the ground on an e-bike ranked quite low on the list.

I relived the events to attempt to piece together the abrasions with the likely causes and culprits. It was a fairly easy puzzle to solve. That gash was the gravel, this is where my forearm hit the steel rail, that's the pedals. But what was beginning to concern me was an increasing pain from the top of my right rib cage. That's when I remembered my entire right side had broken my fall. The focus of the pain sensors in my brain shifted from abrasions to more lasting and severe injuries along with a dull ache in my ribs.

As a young lad, my sister told me how easy it was to ride a bike. This couldn't have been further from the truth. I was something of a slow learner. My first attempt saw me crashing headlong into the next door neighbour's fishpond to the delight of a group of onlookers as I emerged coughing out pond water and assorted plants. Other instances gradually mounted, repeatedly jarring my genitals on the bike seat to the point where I wondered if I would ever be able to conceive children. I had no recollection of any sort of pain like this though.

Fearing broken ribs or a punctured lung, I decided to monitor the situation and hope for the best. In hindsight, perhaps taking preventative action to reduce any further impact of the fall may have been a more strategic tactic, but I chose hope instead.

As I emerged from the quiet haven of the lavatory and into the office, questions flew at me from all sides. There was a mixture of concern, joviality and statements of the obvious, like, "Well that was always gonna happen."

The day wore on, and it was reassuringly clear that, although the pain in my right side was nagging, it was probably not fatal. I recalled I had another nine weeks on the bike to look forward to, including riding home that night. Oh goody!

In order to assess the roadworthiness of the bike (not to mention my body), I took it for a short stint along the road. It wasn't too bad. The bike seemed sound, and my body seemed up to the job.

I managed the trip home at the end of the day, and Jo, an excellent interrogator, extracted the blow-by-blow details. Despite being a highly-credentialed theatre nurse, she has skills that are directly transferrable to counter espionage specialising in techniques of interrogation. Both of these skillsets were deployed as soon as she laid eyes on me that night. I was subjected to the application of pain killers, frozen baby peas and detailed questioning as to the pain levels between one to ten. I also became familiar with phrases such as "large hematoma," "pulmonary rigor mortis" and equally baffling medical descriptions of my injuries.

Resigned to the inevitability of the evening ahead, I plied myself with medicinal red wine and did my best to answer the questions as succinctly as I could using a variety of one word answers that essentially meant "yes" or "no." As the evening wore on I could see she was weighing up two options: euthanasia or allowing me to suffer in silence. Thankfully she chose the latter.

After a restless night, I had difficulty determining which side was more painful to lie on. The pain ambush had been skilfully executed. I was thrust into an unwilling conflict of trying to get comfortable and not slipping out of bed due to the many lotions and potions that had been applied to me. At least if I fell out it would be onto the carpet, which was much nicer than the road.

Dawn broke and the full realisation hit me: my body was not normal.

Having experienced numerous physical traumas in my fifty-plus years, I had never experienced anything resembling this pain. Getting out of bed felt like I'd been handcuffed to a chair whilst being expertly punched by a highly-trained boxer or being abducted by vengeful aliens who employed advanced torture equipment. I discovered that a sneezing fit was my worst nightmare, and it seemed to happen with macabre regularity. Perhaps the road authority had used a type of gravel on the roadside that induced sneezing!

It was clear I would not be riding the bike for a while, and that, despite my determination to see out my driving ban with Winny, discretion was the better part of valour. A lift to work and back was my only option.

I hoped the worst of the pain was behind me as I arrived at work, and that I would start to feel better soon. However, the consensus view of the majority of my colleagues was that day two was always worse as far as pain goes! It struck me how amazing it was that I had told only a handful of people about my unfortunate and embarrassing mishap, but everyone in the office seemed to know! My brother even phoned me because he had heard what had happened from someone at the bike shop where I'd purchased the bike almost two years ago. News certainly travels fast around here.

Day two was worse. My left leg had a psychedelic purple bruise, my right thigh was swollen, and my ribs caused me to grunt and contort my face into strange expressions. As the week wore on, the pain gradually improved. Sleeping still resembled a medieval torture chamber, but I was able to get out of bed, albeit painfully. I was not able to ride because if I had another fall, the damage could be really serious, so I accepted Jo's kind offer of a lift to work and a ride home with a colleague for the next two days.

I had now abandoned any prospect of making a profession out of bike riding, or jousting, instead focusing on how I would actually manage surviving the three-month driving ban without a violent, premature death at the hands of a log truck, poisonous snake or—a new addition on the blacklist—a railway crossing.

The nagging thought that perhaps the bike was in the same state of roadworthiness as I was played on my mind. Uncertain thoughts about the mysterious bike seat incident lingered, and I wondered if my confrontation with the railway line had knocked anything loose. The thought of a wheel coming off during the descent from Tower Hill, or brake failure didn't bear thinking about, so I booked into the bike shop to have it checked for soundness before my daily exodus resumed. This gave me time to recover from the fall and restore some confidence.

When the bike came back with a clean bill of health from the mechanic, I cautiously took it for short trips to collect a takeaway coffee on the weekend. I gingerly rode passed the open garages along the way. I took great care to avoid risking further incident and reinjuring my improving but still very sore ribs. But at least I was able to ride.

There was nothing else for it but to take stock, learn from the experience and get off and walk across that damn railway line. I found out later that many riders had come to grief on that railway crossing. Injuries ranged from broken ribs to near fatalities. This made me feel less inept as a rider and more in keeping with the long list of victims who, blissfully unaware of the dangers associated with this particular crossing, all described it as "a killer."

I felt I should warn unsuspecting riders that they were approaching a "killer" crossing. Suggestion box thoughts to the authorities included signage stating "Killer Crossing Ahead" painted in the bike lane, or "Scenic Lookout for Those Taking Morbid Fascination in Others' Misfortune." If the reports were anything to go by, perhaps coin-operated long-range binoculars could be installed at strategic viewpoints to turn a modest profit. Recliner chairs alongside the path installed for the comfort of onlookers? Why not?

Needless to say, I was slightly hacked off. I accept the risks of taking to the roads on a pedal bike, but it cuts both ways, so authorities should fix this bloody crossing especially if there is a known history of accidents. They should at least consider my helpful signage suggestions. Or carpet it.

Still, next week was next week, and it would come soon enough. As the bike was given the all-clear and repairs were completed, there was no reason why, with my hard-won experience and ever-increasing list of things not to do, my new life could return to abnormal.

8
Rona and La Niña Buddy Up

Just as everyone thought things in Victoria were returning to some sort of normality, our old mate "Rona" (coronavirus—we shorten everything in Australia) decided otherwise. In February, travellers who returned from overseas entered Australia in increasing numbers and brought more of the virus as well as a new variant. For whatever reason, the hotel quarantine program had not managed to contain the virus, and it escaped into the community. The premier of Victoria called a snap five-day lockdown that affected everyone in the state.

He reinstituted the "four reasons to leave home" rule. The only reason we could leave home was to undertake essential work (my work in government was considered essential), buy groceries, exercise (limited to two hours within five kilometres of your home) and provide essential care to somebody. This was a disaster for many Victorians. Holidays cancelled, events postponed, restaurants closed (except for takeaway) and back to home-schooling and working from home. It wasn't too bad for me, but I really felt for so many people whose lives and livelihoods were turned upside down again.

Having fallen off the bike, I needed time to recover from my injuries. Apart from the many and varied restrictions which curtailed most of our daily activities and lifestyles, a stint working from home with no daily two-wheeled commute was a positive for me in an otherwise unpleasant situation.

When I had the bike checked over to make sure no essential parts were damaged or missing in action, I asked them to be very thorough. Having something of a vivid imagination, I had conjured up all manner of unlikely and far-fetched ways I could come to grief again. Exploding tyres, being impaled by a wheel spoke or blinded by the bell coming loose and flying into my face all came to mind. Unlikely, but not entirely outside the realm of possibility. Remarkably, the bike had come through in generally good shape. All it needed was a handlebar and brake adjustment, a few screws to tighten the coffee cup holder (most important) and a bit of a clean-up. I made particular mention of ensuring the bike seat was firmly in place this time.

It was mid-February. La Niña had buddied up with Rona, and they both seemed content to stick around for a while. This meant that not only was it a cool, wet summer, there was an invisible virus which was becoming quite adept at reinventing itself to avoid detection. Add in the restrictions and the cancellation of most things resembling fun and enjoyment, and I was beginning to think that 2021 might be a disappointment—a bit like sprouts or warm beer—but surely it couldn't be worse than 2020!

As the premier said I was allowed to exercise for two hours a day, I took the opportunity to get back on the bike to regain some confidence and get a break from the ride-on mowers which everyone in Koroit had taken to (presumably to relieve their boredom). The travel restrictions meant it was unlikely I would encounter anything too drastic out on the roads because everyone seemed to be inside watching *M*A*S*H* reruns.

My injuries from the fall were still a bit painful on Saturday, but I had to keep at it. As I rode through the village, I couldn't help noticing the number of children mowing lawns on a ride-on. *They are obviously put into training at quite a young age around here*, I thought. They manoeuvred up and back and around tight corners with precision, skilfully navigating the various obstacles in their path. It struck me that if ride-on mowing were ever made an Olympic sport, the locals would make a good fist of winning a medal. Perhaps this is why they were put into training at such a young age—it pays to be prepared! I had visions of parents looking on with pride at their talented offspring on the winner's podium.

"I'd like to thank my dad for taking me to ride-on practice and mum for making the sponge cakes for the ride-on club," the gold medallist might say tearfully. Adding in good humour "without mum washing our club gear after practice and competitions every week, we'd have been lost and probably all smell a bit iffy."

Riding at leisure today, I happened to notice some information plaques recounting the history of Koroit Station. Intrigued by how a septic tank could possibly be as infamous as to rate a mention in the annals of the Koroit Station, I read with amusement. Apparently, in its day this septic tank was thought to be the largest one in the southern hemisphere! For some reason the plaque quotes the *Koroit Sentinel* and *Tower Hill Advocate* newspapers of 1907 (which I guess the historians must have liked and decided to include in the piece): "The ladies' and gentlemen's lavatories are said to be the most complete in the state outside of Melbourne." High praise indeed. "A septic tank is to be constructed in conjunction with them." Things must have been pretty quiet in Koroit in 1907 if a highlight of the year was the lavatories and a particularly newsworthy septic tank. "Festivities to celebrate the opening of the new station were, however, delayed by the innovative, but incomplete septic system," it continued. How the world has changed. I doubt that even the slowest of news days in 2021 would feature the innovation of a septic system and how it could delay festivities! *What sort of festivities would be delayed by an incomplete septic tank?* I wondered.

Reading with increased amusement, it went on to explain, "The railways were justly proud of the new system and delayed celebrations till all was complete. A glimpse at the size of the new large urinal gave some indication of the numbers frequenting the station." In conclusion, the plaque emphatically stated that the urinal "ran the entire width of the building." The local council at the time, probably quite wisely, considered and rejected the temptation to emulate other parts of Australia in having a "big something." In Australia we have "big koalas," "big lobsters" and "big pineapples" in areas known for such things. These structures made from all sorts of strange materials mark entry points to the various towns. I doubt anyone would think it a good idea for Koroit to be known for the "big septic tank." No, that wouldn't do at all. Without wishing to make light of this architectural and innovative masterpiece, I wondered at the fascination of the Victorians who decided that this item was up there with the Roman Coliseum and Hadrian's Wall. The tongue-in-cheek nature of the plaque was not lost on me, and I continued my leisurely ride as I chuckled.

Having spotted some rather fetching profiteroles in the local bakery, I decided to stop there on the way home. With three of said items neatly packed into the saddlebags of the bike, I climbed aboard to ride home and wait out the first day of the new lockdown. As I was about to set off, an elderly gent with a walking stick approached me. He stopped and regarded me suspiciously.

"You local?" he asked in a gravelly Aussie drawl.

Having lived here for almost three months, I thought I probably qualified as a temporary resident and responded, "Sort of."

His eyes narrowed and he frowned, "Nearly got meself run over last week by one of these bloody things."

"Oh really?"

"Wasn't you, was ut?"

"No, not me," I said.

"This electric?" he said, continuing the interrogation.

"Yes, but it wasn't me."

"Mmm, looked like you."

I had encountered several hazards and strange twists of fortune in the past few weeks, but this one was totally unexpected. The wizen-faced local wielding a walking stick with an obvious grievance was now the latest. Not wishing to anger the gentlemen further for fear of being poked at close range in my sore ribs, I made my polite exit.

"No, really, it wasn't me."

Unconvinced, he walked off pointing his walking stick at me. "Yeah, well look where you're going next time," he growled. "Bloody things should be outlawed."

This argument was a lost cause. I was unfairly incriminated, so I rode home to *M*A*S*H* reruns and slightly squashed profiteroles.

Sunday seemed like a good time to hop on the bike and do some more riding. Koroit is a pretty quiet and peaceful place even at the busiest times of the day, but today it was like a ghost town. It reminded me of a day in my childhood when I was watching the local football Grand Final in Port Fairy. Grand Final day in the country was a big deal back then, and folks attended from far and wide. This was about forty years ago, but today was no different; literally everyone in town was at the football. I was bored with the game as South Warrnambool (my team) was being flogged to death by Koroit (again!), so I decided there were more interesting things to do than sit through another depressing defeat. I walked into Port Fairy from the grounds to see what else may be going on.

The place was literally deserted. Shops all closed, nobody to be seen anywhere. It was eerie and almost as dull as the football match. My vivid boyhood imagination kicked in, and I wondered if perhaps there was an impending alien attack. Those not at the football were huddling together in the laundry not daring to venture out for fear of being abducted.

This particular Sunday in lockdown was a bit like that Grand Final Sunday forty years previous. There was no traffic on the streets and not a soul walking around. The snap lockdown had the desired effect as people were dutifully observing the rules, though there were a few passers-by who had ventured onto the rail trail to get some exercise.

A lot of people in rural Victoria were indignant about being locked down again, as COVID-19 cases had been at zero for a number of months. The new cluster in Melbourne had caused the sudden lockdown, and many country folk were hacked off at being locked down because of a small cluster of city slickers. There were reports of huge lines of traffic as Melbournians fled the metropolitan area on the Friday night after the lockdown was announced, so I wondered what the point of it all was. However, my view was we were all in this together, and if the pandemic was ever to be brought under control, it was one in all in. It was just something we had to do. I must say that as unpopular and devastating to businesses as lockdowns are, they kept Australia in much better shape with case numbers than many other parts of the world. Living in Australia during the pandemic was one of the safest places in the world, and living in the country was even better.

I encountered some dog walkers on my ride, and all were wearing masks (not the dogs—they were not at all fussed by the lockdown). The few people I encountered were in good spirits and getting on with things. They greeted me cheerfully as I rode past, along with around eight million flies who decided to keep me company.

I suspected that the five day lockdown was probably likely to be longer, but I wasn't sure. If it were only a short lockdown, I may have found myself riding to work again, so I headed home to plan for this possibility. I had to meticulously study the forecast, choose appropriate clothing and make a host of other preparations that riding to work posed.

9

Enter Neville the Chihuahua

The inevitability of being chased and/or bitten by a dog while riding was one I took seriously. There was a good chance it could happen. Prior to owning dogs, I didn't understand people's fascination and love affair with them. I'd also met some nasty ones. Cats, on the other hand, were smaller and much more manageable. When I moved from Australia to live in England in 1990 I had a cat called Maynard. Moving to England was something I passionately wanted to do. I lived and worked in East Anglia and eventually got married there. Returning to Australia in 2005 to be nearer to my aging parents (who have both sadly passed on), and with the move my marriage broke down. My wife's parents in England were also elderly so she stayed to be with them which I completely understood, they were my adopted parents and I loved them too. So we were torn. We tried a long distance marriage for a while but it proved too much so we parted. When I met Jo, the package deal that she came with was her beloved boy dog Jaspar. Jaspar was a big, goofy, smiling white Labrador who was irresistibly loveable.

Not long after we first met, Jo invited me to her house in Adelaide. I drove to Mount Gambier, just across the South Australian border, and caught the Regional Express flight to Adelaide whilst Jo was at work. When I arrived at her house alone, Jaspar stared at me quizzically through the flywire door. He didn't bark, just stared at me. I wasn't sure if it was safe to introduce myself, as I wasn't able to read his mood, so we just kept up this strange standoff for the afternoon until Jo came home. Finally, we were formally introduced, and it was an instant boy dog, alpha male bonding scenario. I decided to cement the relationship by giving him a lamb chop, which he accepted gratefully, and immediately went off to bury it in his hidden stash of other takeaway snacks and precious oddments. We never looked back.

When Jo left her job to come to live in Warrnambool with me, of course Jaspar came, too, and settled right in to his new home, new life and adopted father. These days, some years after dear old Jaspar passed away at the respectable age of fifteen, we now have three Labrador girls, and I wouldn't have it any other way.

However, I have had many encounters with all sorts of dogs on the bike.

On the way to the entrance to the rail trail, there are two characters who live behind a high-wire fenced property on the outskirts of town. They always lie in wait for my passing and rush toward the fence barking furiously when I approach. The big guy, an Irish wolfhound, has a formidably deep woof which would be audible over a jumbo jet! He scared the daylights out of me as I passed the first time. Not knowing how secure the fencing was at the property, I high-tailed past with visions of him loping after me in hot pursuit. His partner in crime, a Border collie, is the scout who keeps watch and sounds the alarm and call to arms to ambush unsuspecting passers-by. This guy was fast asleep as I rode past one Sunday afternoon, and upon hearing me pass or catching my scent, shot up in the air, furious with himself for being asleep on the job. The wolfhound heard the alarm and lumbered after him, barking ravenously. They both saw me off in fine style. It became a regular event that was a highlight of my ride home.

One Saturday morning ride, a chap was out to buy the paper and walk his dog quietly along the main street of Koroit. Apparently, the dog decided I was an idiot and suddenly snapped at me before resuming its morning walk as if nothing out of the ordinary had even happened.

When I encountered dogs on the rail trail, which I often did on weekends, their owners would always stop and put their companions on a lead obligingly. So if you are frightened of dogs, you have nothing to fear from them on the rail trail (from my experience, anyway).

It was usually the little dogs that gave me trouble. Little dogs have attitude, which they probably need to survive getting pushed around all the time by bigger dogs. It's hard to believe that all breeds of dog apparently descended from an ancient, now extinct wolf species. Breeding and cross-breeding over thousands of years has resulted in all shapes and sizes of modern-day dogs, some of which bear no resemblance whatsoever to a wolf. I initially wondered what the attraction was for a wolf to give up its natural environment and hunting life for a cushy domesticated life. But then again, I can imagine the appeal of a regular meal, affection, safety and shelter from the elements. Humans are the same. We have adapted our modern-day life from the hunter/gatherers we once were. But the instincts are still clearly there. Although "man's best friend" is just that, they are instinctive creatures, and this was always on my mind when riding about.

A guy was walking his little dog on a lead toward me on the trail one day. Out of nowhere the dog took a sudden dislike toward me and started straining at the leash in earnest to have a piece of me. The bloke just kept walking as if nothing was happening while the dog did its darndest to bite me. I managed to get away with my limbs intact, but the little guy was still barking and snapping after I rode off. Whatever had wound him up forced him to follow his instincts.

Our dogs had settled seamlessly into our new temporary home, and they particularly enjoyed their evening walk past the sheep paddocks at the front of our house. The sheep initially regarded them with great caution, only to realise after a short time that these three Labradors were tame enough and were only interested in sniffing every damn thing they went past. Our evening walks are the highlight of their day. It is particularly important to a Labrador to identify particular odours along the way. If we encountered a wet mark on a fence post, I would say, "Girls, it's a dog," to which they would look up at me as if I were a frustrating moron.

"Yes Dad, but what kind of dog?"

With this instinctive character trait in mind, walking our dogs takes three times longer than any usual walk, as we have to stop to sniff out any potential food morsel or dust particle that had come into contact with something edible.

Whilst riding, some dogs regarded me with complete indifference, others took an immediate umbrage to either me, Winny or both. Again it was usually the smaller dogs that saw me as fair game despite the unfair size and weight advantage I had. So watch the little ones when you are riding!

Neville the Chihuahua was a repeat offender. He must have lived nearby, as I encountered him regularly and heard his owner refer to him as Neville. This guy was fearless. He would race after me at twice the speed that was natural for his stubby legs, determined to eat my bike. One morning I awoke to a huge commotion. Neville had decided that his morning walk was far too dull and had wandered into our front garden for a change of scenery. Our dogs immediately responded with the charge of the light brigade toward the side gate, and as I arrived to see what on earth was going on, Neville was goading them through the slats in the gate. The conversation went something like this:

"Three hairy Labradors, is it?! Think you're funny, do ya? You're not even from Koroit."

"Hairy? We'll give you hairy you little shit! Come in here and say that!"

By the time I got there the argument was in full flow. Neville was fearlessly snapping through our gate at the out of towners and our three giving him absolute what-for at having the impertinence to come anywhere near "our house." Neville's apologetic owner explained that their friends had previously lived here, and Neville clearly thought this was part of his patch. Trying to calm the situation to avoid a three-on-one dog sparring session at 7:30 a.m., I reassured Neville's mum that everything was fine and no damage done. Our respective dogs were less conciliatory and continued shouting back at each other.

"Wanna go on with it, com'on!"

They smiled and wagged their tails in anticipation and complete and utter enjoyment. "Stop laughing you three, it's not funny" I told them, "and you as well Neville ya little trouble maker!" Neville walked off jauntily quite chuffed with himself as they went on their merry way.

Jo came out and said, "What on earth was all that about?"

"That," I explained, "was Neville the Chihuahua."

10

On the Road Again

The weather had finally warmed up to coincide with the end of the five-day lockdown. COVID-19 cases in Australia were very low compared to much of the world, and the "circuit breaker" lockdown worked, and the cases soon came back to zero. As the lockdown ended, so did working from home, so I was back on the bike.

It was mid-February. Having mostly recovered from the fall at the railway crossing, it was time to get back on the road again. The morning routine went something like this: Muesli bar? Check. Laptop? Check. Wallet and keys? Check. Water? Check. And so on. Hang on, phone? No, it's in my pocket; OK, let's go, let's go. As I have explained, it is extremely inconvenient to leave something behind. It was good discipline for me to be organised for work as that was a part of my daily routine which was previously lacking. I paid dearly for forgetting my wallet one day and had the embarrassing situation of having to borrow money to buy some lunch!

With the song "On the Road Again" as an earworm, I set off down the rail trail to get to work. The morning was beautiful. Greeted by a stunning sunrise that promised a warm day ahead, I set off along the rail trail through the fields of almost golden pasture which were browning in the late summer sun that had finally arrived. La Niña and Rona were taking a breather.

As I rode down the Tower Hill section, I heard something go *ping!* Thinking it was probably just a stone, I carried on. I reached the bottom of the hill and stopped for a drink as I usually did in the same spot under the trees. I attempted to stand the bike on its foot stand. The foot stand has a "foot" piece attached to the metal stand to help the bike stand up, but it was missing; there was just a straight metal rod. I guess that's what I heard go *ping!* earlier. This wasn't a huge inconvenience, but it made me wonder what else might fly off on my travels. Any confidence in the structural integrity of the bike with its "clean bill of health" from the bike repair chappies suddenly disappeared like La Niña and Rona. If that part had simply fallen off, who's to say what else might fall off during the 35 km/h descent of Tower Hill? It was similar to the bike seat incident, which caused a further twist in unpredictable hazards associated with being entirely dependent on a bike for transport. I sincerely hoped that the manufacturers of e-bikes were not involved in the space program. Thankfully, no other essential parts came adrift on the way to work, and I made the journey safely without incident.

The afternoon ride home was delightful, and the warm sunshine and gentle breeze made for a particularly pleasant ride. It made me think of the many characters who must have taken the train ride along the very corridor

I was riding and what the landscape looked like when the railway was built in Victorian times.

There is a lovely remnant of the lava formation from when Tower Hill erupted in the Illowa section of the trail. Some of the stone has been quarried, but the layers of volcanic rock are clearly visible as a stunning reminder of years gone by.

The Port Fairy-Warrnambool Rail Trail website has some great historical information about the railway and the development of the trail which is well worth a read. It talks about the creation of the railway and how the trail was built. I was actually involved in planning the trail through my work at the local council, and it was ironic that I had never used it until now.

I made a mental note to search for the foot part of the kickstand along the trail as I returned. I could vaguely remember where I had heard the *ping!* as it came off. With the afternoon sun in my eyes, I strained my vision to see if it was still on the path. Sure enough, there it was. Excellent! Another small screw had gradually worked loose and fallen out allowing it to simply drop off. Despite being mechanically challenged, its reinstatement was something that even I could manage.

The next two days were forecast to be hot, windy and forty degrees, the antithesis of the weather during that day's ride home. The heat posed a fresh challenge, and the wind was something else! Imagine an enormous hair dryer aimed directly at your face for an hour. If that was not enough, the hot north windy weather took the level of difficulty up when riding the e-bike. Winny was quite heavy and had a tendency to be caught by sudden wind gusts which cause her to veer suddenly if I was not concentrating. I wasn't entirely sure, but I suspected this was why serious cyclists wore Lycra and shaved their legs to reduce wind resistance. I would employ neither of these measures. I didn't exactly have the figure to wear body-hugging attire, and it was not exactly business attire anyway. I also doubted I could find an industrial scale razor capable of shaving my somewhat hirsute legs. My riding attire was anything but body hugging. The fluoro jacket, which claimed to be water resistant, was actually like a sponge and somewhat resembled a small doona. The aerodynamic qualities of me on the bike were hardly comparable to Donald Campbell's sleek Bluebird high-speed motor boat. I was more akin to a London double-decker bus. That I was roughly the same colour rounded the likeness.

The weather lived up to the forecasters' predictions over the next few days. A furnace wind blew at me as I rode into it. The bike veered one way then another as the wind gusts inflated my clothing like a sail. I could, of course, invest in more wind-resistant outer garments but opted to stay with the high-visibility option for safety's sake and fight the wind with my bare hands. It was a bit like turbulence on an aircraft which would shake the bike violently at the slightest gust. This added what seemed like many additional kilometres to the ride, as I zigzagged all the way. On a positive note, the additional distance undoubtedly improved my fitness, strength and riding skill. It was never my intention to take bike riding to a higher level, but my experience certainly improved my basic skill of staying on the bike.

On the Road Again

Of course, I had other options for commuting. Co-workers offered lifts regularly, and I could catch the bus if I wanted to. But I stubbornly resisted these easy alternatives because I was determined to see out the challenge and stay with Winny. It was a bit of a pact I had made with myself, and getting a lift gave me a sense of guilt for some stupid reason.

Along with the heat came sweat. It stung my eyes and slid ticklishly down my back to impossible places to reach or scratch. Not only would I arrive home with the bloodshot eyes of a three-day bender, but the Labradors took particular interest in my legs, licking off the beads of sweat to aid their apparent salt deficiency. With my hair standing on end after being soaked in sweat and then blow-dried by a hot north wind, I was a fearsome sight. I could get a part in Game of Thrones. Without make-up.

With the pandemic still raging around the world, home delivery of goods was prevalent, and we had taken full advantage of having things delivered rather than going to the shops as often or at all. One evening shortly after arriving home, there was a knock at the door. I was freshly off of my bike from the ride home, so when I opened the door the delivery man jumped back in alarm, clearly shocked at the bloodshot-eyed, wild-haired beast/man before him. Mad professor with a hint of Dracula was probably not what he was anticipating when delivering two cases of red wine to the sleepy town of Koroit. I imagined that our address would be listed on some whiteboard in a delivery depot to warn unsuspecting delivery drivers that the guy at this address was into some sort of weird shit and to approach with caution. I thanked him for the wine, and he took a furtive look back as he walked back to the van, shaking his head in disbelief.

Riding in the heat was not much fun, but as I rode along on the second day of the heatwave, the hot weather reminded me of a time when Mum and I went to Scotland together. Mum was fascinated with anything to do with Scotland and decided to come over to the UK to visit me for my birthday one year. Naturally, I took her to Scotland. The weather on the Isle of Skye was actually hot, which is, of course, unusual for up there. The stunning scenery was accentuated by this lovely hot day of about thirty degrees. The locals said it was a scorcher.

Mum also enjoyed a glass of Scotch. Pubs had restricted hours in those days, so I took her to the ferry terminal on the island where there was a bar for the passengers to have a drink. The ferry was due and the place was packed. Mum was never much of a drinker, but she was beside herself when I presented her with a glass of Scotch. Here she was in Scotland having a Scotch surrounded by locals. She was in her element.

She was a wee bit tipsy when she finished, so I decided to get her another just for the theatre of it all. The bar area was heaving. Thirsty travellers were lined up three deep at the bar, and it took ages to get served, which was OK as it would give Mum a bit of time to sober up after Scotch number one. The guy in front of me had ordered a pint, and the red-faced barman was most apologetic in how long it was taking to pour. The beer was literally trickling into the glass, and he kept saying in a broad Scottish accent, "I'm so sorry. It's the heat, it's affecting the gas." When the glass was finally full, the chap thanked the barman, paid and left. The guy beside had witnessed the scene, and he was next. When asked what he would like to drink, he loudly declared, "Fifteen pints of lager please!"

"I beg your pardon?" the barman said, staring at him in horror. He seemed ready to burst into tears.

"Fifteen pints of lager!" the chap said even louder.

The barman was completely shattered by the thought of it all and quietly cursed the heat and for getting out of bed that day. The customer laughed and said, "I'm only joking, I'll just have an orange juice." The barman was so relieved he threw his arms in the air, clutched his chest and shouted in a very Scottish accent, "Oh Christ, my heart stopped!" We all laughed, and I ordered Mum another large Scotch which was served in what looked like a Vegemite jar. By the end of it all, she was well sloshed. She still talked to anyone who would listen about her Scottish trip and this "hot day" in Scotland many years after.

I worked with a Scottish girl back in Australia, and I prided myself on having a decent impersonation of a Scottish accent, which I told her this story in. Expecting her to be suitably impressed, she said, "Och Glenn, that is the worst Scottish accent I have EVER heard"!

Reaching home, a cool change and sea breeze thankfully arrived. At least the rest of the week would be more bearable for riding. The temperature dropped from 42°C at 4:00 p.m. to 26°C by 6:00 p.m. everything and everyone breathed a heavy sigh of relief. The Labradors picked up their favourite balls for chasing and waited at the back door expectantly as a reminder that with the cool of the evening, the nightly ball chasing ritual could now resume.

11

Riding the Breeze

It was the twentieth of February, a Saturday, and it had been a month since I started riding everywhere. Looking back at what had happened in just one month, I had no doubt I'd have more stories to tell at the end of this.

In keeping with tradition, I used the weekends to keep my fitness up and explore other parts of the area. I rode down to the recreation reserve, formally known as Victoria Park, where there was a local cricket match under way. I heard excited shouts of "Catch it!" and "Good ball, Bobby!" with the participants enthusiastically engaged in the match. Sporting events had been allowed to resume at the end of the "circuit breaker" lockdown, and the cricketers relished being able to play again instead of mowing lawns. One slightly portly chap was batting. Despite an unlikely physique for playing sport (save perhaps darts), he was whacking the ball to all parts of the ground with consummate ease. He had no doubt modelled himself on David Boon, the former Australian cricket team opening batsman, who was of a similar size. This guy was almost as effective a batsman as Boony too.

A wide ball outside the off stump was handsomely dispatched to the boundary, followed by a second which cleared the fence landing not far from where I was watching. Having already had some close shaves with death on the bike, I decided that being struck on the head by a David Boon-style lofted drive was an unnecessary risk—crash helmet or not. So I left the cricketers to it and set off through the village to pick up the rail trail and continue my training. I headed toward Port Fairy where there were fewer people on the trail than the previous lockdown weekend. People were getting on with their usual weekend activities.

There was a black car parked on the side of the road at the crossing, and two ladies stood there chatting about something or other. As I approached one of the ladies, she asked, "Goin' through to Port Fairy are ya?"

"No, just a short ride today," I responded and carried on leaving them deep in conversation.

Port Fairy is a beautiful little town. It is the quintessential seaside village of this part of the world. Originally called Belfast by the Irish who went to live there in the 1800s, it was then a remote whaling station inhabited by hardy folk making a sparse living in what must have been the arse end of Christendom in those days. Today, Port Fairy is significantly more gentrified, with expensive holiday homes blended with well-preserved Victorian architecture. There are countless latte sipping folk in trendy restaurants, stunning white sand beaches and breathtaking scenery that makes it a seriously popular place for holidaymakers and day trippers.

In summer, the population expands from about two thousand people to somewhere near twenty thousand. Many popular events like music, food and wine festivals attract visitors in the thousands. I was a recent resident of Port Fairy and looked forward to returning once the new house was built, so I know its great appeal. If you have been there, you will understand. I must say, though, that my favourite time of the year in Port Fairy is the winter when the locals have the place to themselves.

After about an hour, I headed back to Koroit the way I had come. The two ladies were still in exactly the same position as when I had left them, and still fully engrossed in conversation. It was hard to imagine what topic had led to one of them pulling off the road for a chat in the middle of nowhere. The demise of Donald Trump? The outrageous price of avocadoes thanks to the La Niña summer or some clandestine matter that could only be discussed on a roadside crossing of the rail trail out of earshot. Whatever it was, it managed to keep them interested and immobile for at least an hour. I love that country people take pure enjoyment of a random lengthy conversation. They seem to have all the time in the world.

Meanwhile, back at the recreation reserve on the way home, the David Boon lookalike was still batting. The fielding team were looking somewhat tired and despondent as he continued to bat his way frustratingly (for them) to a total that must have been approaching a thousand. It seems that the Koroit boys are pretty decent at cricket as well as football.

Sunday morning was a cool and overcast. The evening before was the first time I had heard crickets—the traditional signal for autumn—for the year. Given that it was two months past the solstice, autumn was definitely approaching. Sunrise was also getting slightly later, which would pose new challenges riding to work, particularly at the end of daylight saving in early April. With my driving ban not expiring until April, riding to work in the dark or partial darkness was not something I looked forward to. Perhaps a short holiday in April might be something to consider to reduce the commute by bike. I would chat to the boss to see if this was OK.

Holidays were in short supply during COVID-19 as most people, myself included, were either locked down or unwilling to go anywhere for fear of catching the virus. So annual leave was building up. My workload had increased significantly, and although I worked from home for part of most days, there was always more to deal with. A holiday seemed completely out of the question.

I was surprised at the sorts of things that were busy during the pandemic. Real estate was going crazy and used car sales were on the up with people (myself included) being suspicious of taking public transport. Bike sales went up for the same reason. Once some restrictions were lifted, construction went crazy and building materials were in short supply. Some industries were doing it really hard, like the holiday industry. Many people had cancelled holidays and, as with me, people had accumulated quite a bit of annual leave, so it was a logical decision to take some if I could.

There was no wind on that Sunday morning ride, which is quite rare on the coast but always nicer to ride in. I passed a lush field of potatoes, which the area is renowned for, and I saw a haze of butterflies milling around the crop, which lifted my spirits. The flowering potatoes were clearly attracting the butterflies and other insects.

There was an enormous black bull with the number 480 painted on it in a paddock right next door to the old Koroit Station. *Was the number to help the farmer identify the animal? Or was 480 its shoe size?* As you can tell, I know nothing about farming. The bull stared at me impassively as I rode past. I was extremely grateful that given his size and whatever the number on his bum meant, he was safely behind a wire fence and not on the loose like the hippy cow in Dennington.

Sunday is theoretically a day of rest, so I only did a short ride mostly for leisure and to pick up some necessities on the way home. As I was coming out of the bakery, the old guy with the walking stick I had met a few days earlier was slowly walking toward me heading in the direction of the supermarket. He stopped, seemed to recognise me and scowled vehemently. Apparently I had made quite an impression on him. Steadying himself to deliver another serve on the ever present threat of e-bikes, he froze. He gently patted his pockets one by one, methodically and with great concentration.

"Bugger it," he said under his breath when he realised his mistake.

He slowly turned around and made his way back in the direction he had come. It occurred to me that it would be a kind gesture to offer him some money to save him walking home to get his wallet, but he seemed to be in no mood to accept charity. There was also the fact that I might open his missed opportunity to lecture me all over again, so I left him to it and rode home.

The lovely Koroit Botanic Gardens are on my route home, so I leaned the bike against a sundial and had a wander around. The gardens are very pleasant, beautifully kept and would be great spot for a picnic or family gathering. There is a barbeque area which has its own shelter, manicured lawns, and a wide variety of large trees, flowers and shrubs. The gardens took full advantage of the rich, volcanic soil in this area. What a treat to have in the "neighbourhood." I was particularly taken with a superb old Moreton Bay Fig tree with a magnificent canopy. It must have been sixty metres high. These trees are native to eastern Australia, but there are some in Warrnambool which the town planners at the time must have taken a shine to. They were usually planted in parks and the thinking behind their use was of a big space tree. A flock of black cockatoos flapped about leisurely, and other brightly-coloured parrots added to the experience.

A young family were walking through the gardens with two small children and drew toward me. The guy was wheeling a bike and started staring admiringly at my bike as I walked it past them. We said a polite hello, and as I rode off he shouted, "Wow, look at how fast he's going and he's hardly even pedalling!" He seemed so impressed by mine that it seemed he might buy one. Little did he know of the adventures and mishaps that one can encounter on one of these.

I stopped at the newsagents on the way home and overheard as I approached a couple of lads chatting in heavy Irish accents. They suddenly stopped and stared at the bike as I wheeled to a stop. Perhaps they had been stranded in Australia with the ban on international travel or maybe they were locals, I couldn't tell.

"Dat's a neat bike!" one of them said in his accent. "Look, it even has a slimline electric motor, perfect for pedalling up all deez hills!"

They stared in fascination at it and me and carried on discussing the obvious benefits of e-biking for the "mature gentlemen" (as they put it) as I went inside. They had gone when I came out, but I imagined them still going on about it.

Whilst e-bikes are great (apart from bits inconveniently falling off when I would least expect it), they can also be a bit unpredictable. Sometimes when I really need the motor to kick in, it's stubborn and won't no matter how hard I push the pedals. On other occasions, just touching the pedals sets it off, and I end up spilling my hot morning coffee all over the bike and myself. It can be a bit annoying when using the rail trail, as there are a good many chicanes to negotiate to keep the speed down and probably to keep motorbikes off. I initially tried to develop the skill of slowly riding through them without having to dismount. However, the unpredictable bike motor kicking in at the merest of touch of the pedals would propel me headlong toward the chicane without warning, so I'd have to lunge quickly at the brakes to prevent a collision. One day the bike pulled a spectacular monowheel as I applied brakes, much like a headstrong thoroughbred.

"Whoa! Settle down, Winny, you'll pull me over ya wild beast!"

As I gained experience, I hopped off and walked through, not wanting to suffer any further incidents or injuries. So if you have never ridden an e-bike, watch this aspect when you do ride one.

That afternoon, the sun broke through and the day was warm, so I thought it would be nice to spend time in the garden with a glass of something chilled, hopefully alcoholic. This would deftly defer any thought of the prospect of the week ahead and the commencement of my second month riding to work. So much had happened in a short time. When I told people my licence was suspended and shared stories of my commute, their reactions ranged from incredulous to all out laughter (but mostly laughter). Australians, more than anyone else, seem to find great humour in the misfortunes of others.

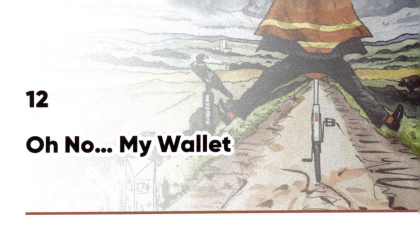

12

Oh No... My Wallet

You know that sinking feeling when you can't find something? It happened to me the next day. As I readied myself for the ride to work, the sky was beginning to lighten, and a blazing red sunrise greeted me on the rail trail. Usually, a bright red sunrise forewarns of rain, unlike red sunsets which usually promise nice weather the next day. This sunrise, however, was a portent of something else, something bad. Something like losing my wallet.

The trip to work was fine, although it was a bit windy and quite cold. The temperature leaving home was a balmy five degrees, but it was bearable. It also gave me the chance to take the wetlands route for a change as the snakes would be huddled safely in their warm holes watching telly and not terrorising blokes trying to get to work on an e-bike.

I parked the bike in the shed and gathered the things I needed for the day ahead: keys, phone and wallet. Wallet? Check pockets, not there. Jacket? Nope. Saddlebags must be. No. Zip pockets of saddlebags, no. Pockets again, no, saddlebags again no. Oh no! I was sure my wallet was in my pocket when leaving home, but I'm usually in a hurry to beat the cow rush hour.

Clinging to the remote but last remaining possibility that my wallet was still at home, I rang Jo who, thankfully, had the day off.

"Did I leave my wallet at home?" I pleaded with desperate hope when she answered.

The inevitable questions, "Did you have it when you left? Where do you keep it on the ride? Are you sure it's not in your pocket?" ensued. She instigated a thorough search but came up with nothing.

I immediately blocked access to the credit and debit cards, so I was skint. Well, not entirely. I had fifty-five cents in loose change in my desk drawer, but this would not extend to the purchase of barbequed chicken and chips or even an apple. Jo offered to drive some of the way I had come to see if it was lying on the road somewhere, but I was already sure it must have fallen out of my pockets, so finding it by car was a longshot.

Losing your wallet is really bad news.

Not only did I have no money, but I also had no ability to withdraw money without a card. My bank did not have a feature to withdraw money using a smartphone and without a debit or credit card, I was without any means of doing so. It also meant the absolute pain of having to not only block the cards but to ultimately cancel the cards, reorder them and wait up to two weeks until they arrived!

There were other inconveniences as well. My work access card was in my wallet, so not only was I not able to enter the building, but I also couldn't use the printers and so many other things that required the access card. My Medicare card was in the wallet, so best not to get sick. Numerous other things that came in handy were in there as well. I had another "oh no" moment as the magnitude of inconvenience set in.

It wasn't so much the cash element, as, like most people these days, I didn't carry much around. I had about thirty-five dollars in it, which is almost enough to buy an avocado or some garlic, the price of which had skyrocketed during the pandemic. I would probably never find out if this was the case, as I had to ration my expenditure to the bare necessities of life and my daily cash allowance probably wouldn't stretch to such luxuries.

I waited for ages for someone to let me into the building, so I began to work through the items I needed to replace if Jo's search for the wallet was unfruitful. After about an hour, she called to report the inevitable: no sign of it anywhere. Damn and blast. I asked her to bring me some cash so I could at least eat lunch.

The whole sorry affair put me in mind of the old guy on the weekend getting to the shops without his wallet. Now I knew how he felt, but I guessed he had simply forgotten his rather than lost it.

There was another slim hope: I might find the wallet on the way home by retracing my route. After a cold morning, the day had warmed up nicely, and that ruled out the wetland section of the ride. If it was lost in the wetlands it was going to stay lost. There was no way I was going home that way on a warm night after the previous unsettling snake encounters!

Getting a replacement access card was straight forward enough, so I was at least able to get in and out of work. I could check my bike saddlebags and jacket again just to make sure I was not having a mental moment that may have been associated with the physical trauma of falling off my bike. Now I was really clutching at straws.

The other aspect to all of this was that the wallet was expensive and had been a birthday gift from Jo. It had my initials embossed on it, which was a nice touch but did not help to identify the owner if it was found. The credit card had my name on it, but there was nothing else with my address in the wallet. Why? Because the only thing with my address on it was my driver's licence! That is, of course, going on the assumption that there are still decent people left in the world who wouldn't take the cash and cards and chuck the wallet into the long grass!

The outlook was not good.

The journey home was long—painfully long! Crawling along the rail trail at a snail's pace, I meticulously retraced my steps. Despite thinking that if I was to find the wallet it would most likely be at the start of the ride, I went slowly from the start and left no stone unturned. After three days (well, it felt like that long), I was halfway home and had found nothing. There was still the most important part of the trail left to ride, so it wasn't completely without hope. I reached the spot where I usually stopped for a drink and to stretch the legs, which was one of the most likely places it may be. Nothing. Even though I was losing hope, I continued searching. Riding up the last part also yielded nothing, so that was probably that; it was lost.

I reached home after the long, fruitless search and carefully discussed the next steps with Jo. I had cancelled and reordered the cards, so I began the process of reinventing the contents of the wallet.

Walking the dogs that night, which was always entertaining, seemed a good option to help clear my head and put the whole sorry saga behind me. That's when I remembered the red sunrise of the morning, and it started to rain. Typical!

Facing a long day and late meeting the next morning, I accepted a lift to work and left the bike at home. My Facebook "lost wallet" plea to the inhabitants of planet Earth yielded nothing, so I accepted the game was finally lost. The prospect of finding my wallet had died a slow death, but it was dead.

The morning at work was particularly busy, so I missed the picture text messages from Jo. She called and told me to check my messages, and there it was staring at me—my wallet. Impossible! Had it been handed in? Remarkable.

Whilst this was excellent news, Jo revealed the true circumstances which put something of a new twist on matters. She decided to search through the saddlebags on the bike and, lo and behold, found the wallet! I was embarrassed and had to admit that this was incontrovertible proof that men really do only have "a boys look" for things. This was simply impossible. I had searched that damn bag countless times. It bloody well wasn't there. Never in my wildest dreams had it occurred to me that it was there all along.

In one way it was great to get it back, as at least I still had the gift Jo had given me and it wasn't laying in some bush on the rail trail bereft of its contents to slowly disintegrate. But it was proof positive that my powers of deduction were remedial or at the very least typical for a bloke, with the resultant blow to my male pride and credibility. Not only that, but I had also cancelled everything, so getting the wallet back was something of a pyrrhic victory.

I wondered at the mystical powers of this wallet. How had it evaded the most thorough and intensive search? Had it slipped magically into some hidden compartment of the saddlebags unbeknownst to me? Did it have its own powers of invisibility to skilfully avoid detection? All these things had to be considered as possibilities if I was to regain some credibility. I reached the inevitable conclusion that there was no point agonising over how this had all happened. As with many things in life that are sent to try us, it is not the winning that proves the best teacher, rather the losing.

These past few weeks had been nothing if not character-building. If I was still alive and sane at the end of this three months, I would have the wisdom of a saint and could pass a master's of philosophy. In all the commotion, I had also run out of cash, and without cards, I had to ask Jo for an extension to my cash overdraft.

13

Two-Wheeled Weekends

Even with the obvious disadvantages that not being able to drive poses, such as the elements, injuries, various forms of venomous things or predatory animals, there are advantages. Shopping, for instance. Country people are particularly obsessed with the notion that one must park immediately in front of their planned destination. If no parking space is available immediately in front, it is usual and accepted practice to keep driving around and around until a vacant space appears right in front.

Then, of course, a series of mind games takes place where one intimidates a potential competitor out of taking the only available space. Tactics involve a race between who can get to the indicator first, which is the unwritten but accepted rule in car parking etiquette. The first to indicate is simply always awarded the car park with the loser accepting lack of speed and reflexes in applying the indicator, admitting defeat and vowing to be quicker off the mark in future. Other more risky strategies include speeding madly around the block to outpace one's opponent or staring formidably at your adversary to worry them out of it.

Not so on an e-bike. The e-bike shopper or regular pedal bike shopper is afforded the luxury of always being able to park right in front of the shop of choice. There are never any arguments or disagreements and no shortage of places to park your bike. One can easily secure it directly onto a bike rack, light pole or other handy piece of public infrastructure that is useful for bikes in addition to being a lavatory for dogs.

Another important advantage is that parking on the footpath is free and not time limited. This means that the e-bike shopper can browse at a leisurely pace safe in the knowledge that the pesky parking inspector cannot rudely intervene with a parking fine!

The bike doors won't get dinged when parking because there aren't any. You don't pay registration fees or insurance, and tyres are a fraction of the cost. Of course, fuel is considerably cheaper as it's largely last night's dinner.

There are limitations upon what the e-biker can carry home from a shopping trip. It would be impractical to carry a box of vegetables or forty kilos of dry dog food, for example, but I'm sure some have attempted it. Having not done so successfully myself, I would not recommend it. Just imagine the stream of dogs it would attract!

Another minor complexity of e-bike versus car can be found at the footy ground. In this part of the world, most people drive to a football match, park their cars around the boundary fence and hoot their car horns whenever a goal is scored. This is more difficult on an e-bike as sounding the bell doesn't quite have the same effect. So in order to capitalise on the savings I've mentioned, perhaps get a lift to the footy.

Living in the country offers one the perfect opportunity to take advantage of riding to the shops to pick up day-to-day necessities such as saucepan scourers, the newspaper and a coffee. I fully intended to continue this practice once my license was restored. The roads are quiet, and it is quite pleasant to cycle into town to take in some fresh air and check out the local real estate market.

It was the end of February, the twenty-seventh to be precise. The tree-lined streets were becoming decorated with fallen leaves as the many deciduous trees shed their summer coats for the autumn. Autumn is my favourite season of the year. The other seasons have their own appeal—the open fires and windswept landscapes of winter, swimming in the summer, and the colours and smells of spring—but autumn is the one I wait for with excitement. The weather is cooler, with fresh mornings and usually warm, sunny afternoons that are perfect for getting out and about.

I rode into the village as normal on Saturday morning to pick up a coffee and the paper. There was a slight hint of wood smoke in the air from houses that had lit their open fires the night before, which is another thing I like about autumn. Autumn in 2021 was more significant, as it meant that my driving ban was slowly elapsing. My choice of riding, however, had become more appealing as time went on. I told a friend who had also been suspended from driving and took up riding everywhere that I would probably keep riding to work upon occasion.

"Yes, I said that," he replied.

I had some leave approved in April, so my riding to work time was reduced, and I could see some light at the end of the tunnel. I just hoped I wouldn't be faced by a metaphorical train in that tunnel before I was through it. A fitting idea when riding the rail trail.

As COVID-19 restrictions were gradually eased and the vaccine rolled out, life was looking more cheery. I determined to enjoy the weekend and include a ride or two.

The front page of the paper quoted the premier of Victoria stating, "This is far from over," when asked about the pandemic. All the more reason to be grateful for what we've got rather than getting too disheartened by the premier's optimism.

It was a still, overcast day as I set off. I passed the old station in Koroit where the big black bull was standing in his usual spot but facing the other way this time. The letters BB in white capitals were on his shoulder. Naturally, "BB" was for "black bull." Farmers are so imaginative. It didn't explain the number 480, but maybe this was some sort of bovine number plate. Maybe this guy was known as BB480. Yes, that must be it.

I stopped in town on the way and saw a gentleman approaching the supermarket. Upon reaching the front door, he stopped, said, "Need a bloody mask," and turned back to fetch one. Although masks weren't required outdoors anymore, they were still mandatory in certain places such as supermarkets. Knowing only too well how it felt to forget and lose things, he had my every sympathy.

Things were hotting up at the recreation reserve. It was a hive of activity with two cricket games about to be staged this particular Saturday. There is the main oval used for football—usually a one-sided affair in favour of the home team—and another ground behind it used exclusively for cricket. The main footy oval was used for both dependent on the season.

There was no sign of old mate today, so the away team would be in with a chance. The cricketers on the front oval were raucously laughing and cheering a chap who was doing his warm up fielding practice. It was difficult to know what they were laughing at, but my imagination ran wild. I was never a cricketer myself and had only played in social games, so I could imagine the skull duggery that went on in club cricket. We had gotten up to all sorts of mischief and practical jokes on my football team. It was a regular pastime to turn off the away team's hot water or remove all the toilet paper from the toilets. Everything was fair game in country footy, and I saw evidence of this in country cricket.

Two things struck me. There is a sewage pump station nearby the public toilets which I was certain had a television aerial on it! What on earth? Perhaps the water authority chappies would bring along a TV to watch *Judge Judy* or *Dr. Phil* whilst doing whatever it was to the pump station. This is something that until now I had never encountered. Quite inventive though.

The other curious thing about the Koroit Recreation Reserve is the number of dog owners that regularly use the oval to play fetch and run their dogs. This is despite the many signs that say: "No dogs allowed on the ovals by order of the committee of management." Clearly, the committee of management is not a formidable force to be reckoned with. Perhaps the dog walkers were on the committee.

As the sun was peeping out, I turned for home to enjoy whatever the afternoon had in prospect. A demolition crew were hard at work removing what looked like a redundant building of some sort on the outskirts of town. The sign on the van said "Asbestos Removal," and the area was taped off. Probably why the work was being done on a Saturday. Some of the workers were coughing, which was probably unrelated, but helped dispel any future intentions that I would pursue this line of work.

It made me recall the movie *The Wizard of Oz* from the 1930s. Turns out that the snow falling on Dorothy, the Scarecrow, the Cowardly Lion and the Tin Man in the poppy field scene was actually 100% industrial grade asbestos. Amazingly, asbestos was used in many films to replicate snow, including that which was dumped on Bing Crosby in *A White Christmas*. I was also told that some cigarette filters in the 1950s were made from asbestos. Well, they wouldn't catch fire, but it was probably harder to cremate smokers from the '50s.

With all of that in the back of my mind, it was time to ride home before my good mood was ruined by further thoughts of a lung condition.

14

Distractions and Brownie Points

It was early March. The weather had been quite cool over the previous few days, and the weeks were slowly passing. The years though seem to fly past. Perhaps it has something to do with our modern-day lifestyle. Life is full of "stuff" to distract us from the passing of time. There is social media—more like antisocial media, given the rancour online. Mobile phones ring all day and sometimes all night. And emails! Don't get me started on them! I hardly ever get a letter. Birthday cards and Christmas cards are all but a distant memory except for a few traditionalists that carried on the old way of communicating and well wishing.

Utility companies don't send you a bill to tell you your account is due, they send you an email and a text message just in case. One to tell you it's due, one to tell you it's still due and one right at the end in case you just happened to miss the other two. That's service for you! Oh and I love the one at the end to tell you your payment has cleared. How irritating is that?!

What with all of this staring at our phones, is it any wonder people are walking into cars, telephone poles and each other? And if the phone doesn't manage to completely distract us, there are screens appearing everywhere. Advertising appears in streets, on buildings, in shops and waiting rooms. It's exhausting!

These days we all want things instantly. Instant credit, buy now pay later, fast food, the list goes on and on. Being a naturally impatient person, it kind of suits me. But it must be the reason why shops put Easter eggs out for sale on Boxing day, and Christmas carols start playing in the supermarket at the beginning of November just in case people had forgotten about Christmas and needed two months of reminding. No wonder the time flies. By the time we've had our Christmas dinner, it's Easter.

The passage of time has always intrigued me. I find it curious that enjoyable events seem to go quite quickly, whereas unpleasant experiences always take forever. While a three-month driving ban seemed short, it seemed like an eternity at this moment.

When people asked when I was due to get my licence back, I would say, "Next month."

"Gee that's gone quick!" they would invariably say.

But it hadn't for me. Time was moving at a snail's pace.

Perhaps the lack of distraction on the rail trail was the reason. At the start of the work week, I invented new ways of riding to and from work to break things up a bit. In the beginning, I would wear earphones to listen to the radio on my phone. During this middle period, I usually opted for silence to be more aware of the world around me. In fact, I heard it was illegal to ride while wearing headphones. Did the offence come with a three-month riding ban? That would be just the very limit, so I took them off permanently! Trading ABC Radio for the sounds of nature seemed more appropriate, and I was probably safer because I could hear approaching traffic and other potential dangers.

Another thing I noticed was that encountering people I knew when riding was quite different to being on foot. They didn't recognise me. One morning riding to work, I passed a good friend who was out for an early morning walk. I said a cheery good morning and expected, "Oh hi, Glenn, how are you?" and perhaps some small talk about me riding a bike to work. Instead, I got a rather aloof and expressionless "morning" because I was unrecognisable in my elaborate disguise.

On another occasion, a former colleague was walking along with a friend. I called her by name while riding past, but the same thing happened. It seems that wearing a bike helmet and sunglasses renders one anonymous. It's something to be borne in mind if I ever decide to do something wrong.

I am a big believer in the points system. For every bad thing we do in life, we attract points which are deducted by the number of good things we do. Hopefully at the end of it all, we have a positive balance. With all the misadventures on this riding quest, I decided I must not be such a good person to have accumulated so many points of penance. So not only was I potentially getting fitter with all of the riding, but I also made a determined effort to only do nice things to reduce my demerit points. I hoped I could then stay out of danger and be a better person inside as well as outside.

At work, I started paying people compliments and being Glenn the Likeable. I offered to this or do that, helped people carry things and was ultra-polite to square the ledger. I wouldn't say I'm a bad person and think that I am quite well-liked, but this new approach was met with surprise in some cases, as work colleagues seemed to give me a second look at my new-found congeniality. Little did they realise this was just a cunning plan to reduce the likelihood of grisly misfortunes happening to me riding to work. I hoped this was not all in vain, and that the brownie point system still worked even if it was contrived.

One person even commented that I seemed much happier these days and enquired whether I was sleeping better and able to unwind more due to riding to and from work. Whilst I was feeling the mental and physical health benefits of riding, the real reason was much more in the interests of self-preservation. I hoped I would not have to dismiss or severely discipline someone at work, fearing a significant backlash in demerit points that would see something particularly nasty happen to me as a consequence.

It made me consider continuing to ride occasionally once my licence was restored but one thing was definite, I would pay meticulous attention to the speed limit in the future. I vowed to drive in a manner befitting a trip to church. Now there's a thought: going to church must be worth a few points, and there are plenty to choose from around here. I may even consider donating the fifty-five cents in my desk drawer to a worthwhile charity.

Donations may also explain a few things. When we sold the house, I donated quite a bit of stuff to charity to declutter. This possibly explains why I was not gored by the hippy cow, bitten by a snake or hit by a car when I fell off my bike. Clearly, the points gained had reduced my penalty points sufficiently.

It was noticeably darker at 6:45 a.m. on my Tuesday morning commute, and I decided to switch on the bike light for the first time. I arrived at the cow crossing with seconds to spare before the farmer let my bovine friends through, and I pedalled hard down Tower Hill. Although the sky was lightening, I had a difficult time seeing where I was going, but the bike light helped oncoming vehicles see me. The moon was almost full that morning, which helped, but there was a stiff, cold headwind.

The autumn weather was another reason to take some leave from work. When I began my "holiday from driving" in mid-January, the sun was already above the horizon, and the air was warmer. On this particular day, the sun didn't poke out until about 7:20 a.m. The sunrise was also receding by a minute each day, so by the end of March it would be another thirty minutes longer for the sunrise. This required some planning.

There are no lights on the trail, of course, and it can be a bit tricky with ruts, sticks and patches of gravel to look out for. Perhaps an investment in a bigger light was in order? Or maybe I should leave later? I wasn't sure. The other thing to consider would be how the various critters would react to a bright light hurtling down the rail trail. It didn't bear thinking about, so I decided to leave a bit later!

The previous day was also when the first person in our region received their COVID-19 vaccination. There were only eleven active cases in Victoria, and we recorded zero new cases most days. Restrictions were gradually being eased with most state borders reopened, no restriction on travel distances from home and only limited mask wearing. Gradually, the news became less about the pandemic and more about day-to-day matters. Having said that, there were still signs up at restaurants around the village saying "Dinning room closed until restrictions are lifted." It made me wonder whether "dinning" was a reference to dinner—or maybe the din in the room where the noisy patrons ate.

There was a bit of commotion at the office when I arrived. One of the council rangers had been attending livestock at large on the outskirts of Warrnambool, which was not all that common. Local council rangers are called to round up livestock at large and to secure them back in the paddock to ensure the public are not injured or traffic impacted. It turned out that one of the cows had taken a dislike to the ranger, charged at him and hurled him into the air. Everyone was thankful that the ranger suffered only a few minor injuries as well as being quite shaken up by the whole incident.

"Were you wearing a hi-vis vest?" I asked casually later that morning.

"Yes, I was," he replied.

"What colour was it?" I enquired.

The response was, of course: "Red"!

So there it was, red hi-vis vests are a definite no-no when it comes to livestock. Turns out this incident was in a different part of town from the stampede I had been involved in, and he wasn't chased by the same cows who chased me up the road. I decided to note a few things for future reference:

1. Don't try to negotiate with cows. They are probably not interested.

2. If you are wearing red in the vicinity of livestock, remove the item immediately.

3. Definitely ensure you are nice to people and do good deeds to get your points up to survive a rabid livestock encounter.

4. Consider donating more that fifty-five cents to charity.

Jo and I seriously discussed going to church together that Sunday.

On reaching home that night, my replacement credit and debit cards had arrived, so I was able to access funds. This was probably due to accruing enough good behaviour points.

15

The Challenges of the Long Weekend in March

Some people ride to work every day and love doing it, which is understandable, although it did not appeal to me in the dead of winter. With the weather and the dark mornings, I mixed up the trips to work and back a bit for the rest of the week. I caught a lift for two days, rode into work for two and worked from home on Friday, which was ideal. It's how I hoped to spend the rest of my driving suspension, and I felt fortunate to have this flexibility.

The long weekend in March was the halfway point of my two-wheeled sabbatical. Forty-five days had elapsed with no driving, and I still had forty-five days to go. Not that I was counting! This weekend is famous for the Port Fairy Folk Festival, but it was cancelled because of lingering concerns around COVID-19. Although the restrictions were entirely sensible, the weekend seemed strange without the folk fest. Thousands of people from all around the country—in fact, all around the world—descend on little old Port Fairy for the weekend. The festival swells the population from 2,000-ish to around ten times that, even more than the school holidays in summer. The price of accommodation trebles, so tents and caravans pop up in the most outlandish of places, and traders of all kinds have sales beyond any other time of the year. Musicians and fans from around the world spend the weekend revelling and enjoying the music and festivities. But along with the great things the festival offers, there are disadvantages.

My first experience of the modern-day festival as a resident of Port Fairy was a mixture of good and bad. I was breathalysed twice driving home on the Friday night, and my letterbox went missing, only to be found a few days later in the river. I lived by the river, which is tidal, and when I looked out of the lounge window I noticed the letterbox looking back at me from the riverbank at low tide. The next morning at 8:00 a.m., I was breathalysed again. I quipped to the policemen, "Hang on, the pubs aren't even open yet." I was met with steely silence and realised that the police officer probably didn't appreciate my sense of humour.

This reminded me of another instance where humour and police didn't go so well. When I lived in Ely near Cambridge in England, a good mate told me the story of how a bloke he knew lost his licence for drunk driving. He used to ride his motorbike to the village pub for a few pints on a Sunday afternoon. He usually kept himself pretty tidy, but one day he got carried away, had too many and made the stupid mistake of hopping on his motorbike to ride home. The police just happened to be in the area, recognised his bike which had been parked in front of the pub virtually all afternoon and followed him as he rode somewhat unsteadily up the road. When he refused to slow down, they put on the siren, but instead of stopping, he sped up to outrun them. On the outskirts of town, clearly the worse for drink, he lost control of the bike, hit an embankment, fell off and rolled down a grassy hill. When the police caught up with him, he was still laughing uncontrollably.

The police officer was unimpressed, and said, "Have you been drinking, Sir?"

"Of course I've been drinking," he said. "What do you think I am, a stuntman?"

This went over so well that he was locked up for the night and lost his licence for two years for being such an idiot. It's probably a salient lesson. If you are stopped by the police, don't crack any jokes because it probably won't work in your favour.

Having said that, I did encounter a police officer on another long weekend who had an excellent sense of humour. Also while I was living in England, I was lucky enough to take my girlfriend at the time, later to become my wife, to see Elton John at the Royal Albert Hall. It was just him and a piano, which was brilliant. I'd had a couple of drinks but was fine to drive. As I was going around a roundabout, I was pulled over. The police officer came to my window and said, "Did you realise you have a tail light not working?" Back in the 1990s in the UK, the police needed a reason to pull you over.

"Really?" I said. "Thanks for letting me know, Officer."

"Where have you been tonight, and have you been drinking?"

As it was quite late on a Sunday night, there was every chance he thought I might have had a few.

"We've been to the Albert Hall to see Elton John."

As I was speaking, he leaned into the driver's side window to smell my breath.

He smiled and said, "Oh you'll be right then, they water the beer there."

He let me drive off.

During the festival in Port Fairy, streets are closed off and don't even think about getting a parking spot in town. The music side of things, however, is a treat. Being something of a miserable git, I was always glad to see the long line of metal as the various cars and camper vans made their way home on the Monday, allowing the village to get back to its usual tranquil self.

The festival wasn't always like this. It came from very humble beginnings. As a youngster, I recall it being a one-night-only affair with the single marquee touting John Williamson singing his early songs. A far cry from today.

On Saturday, it seemed a good idea to go for a ride in place of taking in the festival. It was a fine sunny day, so off I went. A colleague from work had told me earlier that week that they had seen koalas on the rail trail on the way from Koroit to Port Fairy, so it seemed a good thing to investigate. Koalas are not a common sight here, although I've seen some on Tower Hill. We also have emus there. Whilst they are interesting, they have a tendency to steal your picnic lunch or chase you if they don't like the look of you.

I came across a wallaby right in the centre of town on the way to the rail trail! This was not a common sight either. There are, of course, wallabies who like to race you on the rail trail—well, one at least—but not in the centre of town. This one seemed almost tame and was not in the least bit worried about me as I rode past.

Another thing I had not seen for a while was the vapour trail of a jet. High in the clear blue sky, a jet was making its way north. Since international travel for Australian residents was stopped because of the pandemic, this sight was rare though there was still a handful of domestic flights in the skies. I had not seen evidence of any for some time though. It made me wonder where it was going and why.

I had heard that one airline was offering mystery flights from Melbourne. A limit of 120 travellers were offered gourmet foods whilst en route to a mystery destination. Perhaps this was one of them? I am not fond of flying, so a mystery flight seemed about as much fun as self-isolation or stepping on a LEGO brick in bare feet. But it was each to their own. I would prefer to fetch my letterbox from the river or get breathalysed by a policeman with no sense of humour on the long weekend in March.

The other odd thing about this weekend was that some people in Koroit had decided this would be a good time to put unwanted things on the nature strip to be picked up and taken away by the anticipated influx of visitors looking for a freebie. I was new to Koroit, so I wondered if this was an annual ritual or a one-off. I made note to ride past the next day to see if the venture was successful; we certainly could use a declutter in readiness for the move back to Port Fairy in about a year's time once the new house was built.

Tents had been erected on nature strips for free overnight accommodation. Another practice I couldn't imagine doing myself. It was certainly enterprising, if not against what I imagined the local council would encourage since they made a fair amount of revenue in caravan parks. Imagine the romance of camping on a nature strip...

I rode along the rail trail and approached the place where the koala was spotted. And there it was high in a gum tree chewing impassively on a gum leaf. The human eye is designed to detect movement, so although koalas are quite well camouflaged, this one was certainly visible and quite content and chewing away happily. Although some pretty ordinary things had happened over the last 45.5 days (not to be too precise), the chance encounters with wildlife were certainly the highlight for me.

On Sunday morning after church (no, not really, although it did cross my mind), I set off for my ride. I noticed that the paraphernalia left on the nature strip had all gone. Of course, it could have been brought in because nobody wanted any of the items, but I wanted to ride past later just to make sure. So at eleven that warm morning, I made for the rail trail. I noticed an unusual noise, a sort of clacking sound, along the way. They were frogs. Frogs are the fast food equivalent for snakes, so I kept my eyes peeled for the evil beasts, especially given the warmth of the day. Thankfully, nothing of the serpent variety appeared.

The rail trail on the way to Port Fairy was the busiest I had seen it. Lots of people on bikes coming and going in both directions, heaps of dog walkers, all manner of walkers, in fact. Despite there being no folk festival this weekend, Melbourne had emptied itself as it usually did on this March long weekend.

Most people greeted me politely as we passed, although some didn't, which I thought was a bit off-handed. Even a passing dog smiled at me, although perhaps it was having a laugh at my expense. There were people standing at the old Koroit Station as if waiting for a train while they drank cups of tea or coffee. I didn't have the heart to tell them there would be no trains today, or any day, as the rails had been ripped up many years ago. They must have been from Melbourne.

It was getting rather warm, so I turned for home. There is a small supermarket in Koroit, which is handy for day-to-day items, including a small liquor section. As tomorrow was a holiday, it would be nice to have a drink in the garden after my ride, so I popped in to pick up a few beverages. Every time I went to the supermarket there was obscure golden oldies music playing. Yesterday it had been the *Grease* soundtrack, and today it was the Bee Gees. Some of the staff were happily singing along, although their voices were muffled behind their face masks. COVID-19 had some advantages as I rather suspected they could not hit the falsetto notes of the brothers Gibb. So much music these days has a boring, monotonous drum beat and a melody that keeps repeating over and over like the record has become stuck. Not so with the music on offer in this supermarket!

Upon reaching the checkout, I found a lady obliviously chatting away to the checkout operator even though the queue was long.

"It's ridiculous, there are five of them, I demanded an apology!"

The lone checkout person was fully engaged and also oblivious to the growing number of people waiting to be served.

"They can't even go to school," the woman said.

The operator nodded sympathetically.

"Anyway, love, I'll tell you about it next time," the woman said as if the lengthy conversation about whatever it might have been was cut short due to the inconvenient presence of other shoppers.

As I am impatient, my sole mission when shopping is to get in and out in the shortest possible time. The person in front of me struck up a conversation as well.

"How is Dave? Bad year for tomatoes."

While looking for a pencil or something else sharp to poke at them to hurry them along, I was eventually served. The cashier greeted me politely and asked if I needed a bag. I grunted "no," but this caused no offense because wearing a mask in supermarkets was still compulsory and made my grunt somewhat muffled and inoffensive. When the young checkout operator noticed the alcohol, she immediately called over the PA, "Alice to the checkout, please." Alice was deep in conversation at the rear of the store and was not keen to end the conversation. As I approached old age, she finally arrived, greeted me politely and asked if I needed a bag.

"No thank you, I HAVE a bag," I said.

It was clearly visible in my hands the whole time. It's almost as bad as being told to "Have a nice day!" which has been modernised to "Have a great day!" after being served in a shop! I imagined the staff training sessions going something along these lines:

"Now take your time, be friendly to the customers, chat to them, and always ask if they need a bag whether they are holding one or not."

Whilst I am a big supporter of getting rid of single-use plastic—in fact, all plastic—maybe I should get on the front foot and clearly say I have a bag to settle the anxiety of the checkout staff.

As I left the store, the lady behind me, who did not seem in the least bit inconvenienced by how long it had taken to be served, put her bag on the checkout and was politely greeted and asked if she needed a bag.

It's a lovely little supermarket, and the staff are very friendly, but allow a little extra time, and don't worry if you forget your bag.

On the way back, the stuff on the nature strip was gone, but the tents were still there.

Rain was forecast for the holiday Monday. I checked the rain radar on my phone and saw that there was some rain around, but that it looked to be mostly missing us, so I set off for my daily ride. It was mostly drizzle and not particularly cold, so I thought I would be OK.

I'd had vivid dreams the night before. As dreams can be the portent of events to come, certainly from my experience anyway, I was keen to learn what they meant. The first was about a broken tooth, which, according to the dream book on our shelf, signifies insecurity and embarrassment. Insecurity was relevant, especially considering my adventures riding to work. The other dream was about rats, and the book told me it meant upcoming changes in one's life. The rat part bothered me a bit. I like change and believe it is good; after all, it might signify getting my licence back. But after the obstacles riding to work had thrown at me, changes might be for the worse, which didn't appeal.

The rain went from a light drizzle to proper rain, so it was time to head for shelter. As I arrived at the old Koroit Station, I saw some young lads on scooters and skateboards who had the same idea of getting out of the rain. By this time I was well-soaked, and the lads all said hello and showed me some of the tricks that they had learned on their wheels. It passed the time as we all waited for the rain to stop.

Some parents appeared and began to unpack various items, one of which was a fold-out table. One lady unfolded a generously-sized table and lay out an immaculate and quite formal white tablecloth across it.

"Oh this is better. Isn't this better?" an older lady said.

In the fifteen or so minutes that I sat there, she said this same thing at least five times. It was becoming a bit repetitive, so I decided to seek slightly more stimulating conversation. I needed some cash for the week ahead, and the supermarket had the only cash point I had come across. It would be a break in the repetition of "this is better."

The rain showed no signs of easing, but at this point one of the ladies said that the hot food would be here soon! Hot food? This little gathering was obviously pre-planned and well thought through. I agreed with the lady that again said how much better it was and took my leave. I was cold and very wet. Although the thought of gate crashing the little party appealed, I decided to get home without, as the dream suggested, embarrassing myself or listening to "this is better" all afternoon.

At the supermarket, Alice was nowhere to be seen, but there was a long queue at the checkout, naturally. Everyone was politely asked if they needed a bag, but this time I was not asked because I wasn't queuing for anything. The cash machine, however, was one of the slowest I'd encountered.

The song being played over the speakers was about rain and went on melodiously "I Can See Clearly Now," which was apparently released in the 90's. The manager had obviously decided to go more contemporary in the music department and had clearly not been outside that day. The rain had most certainly not gone. In fact, it was worse, so I left.

There are agricultural sheds at the recreation reserve where I stopped to get out of the rain for a bit. The Koroit agricultural show is apparently held there, so there are no shortage of undercover areas. Whilst waiting, a car towing a camper trailer appeared, did a drive around and decided, although it was a likely spot for some free accommodation, it was too wet even for a hardened free camper. A fire truck came in as well for some ridiculous reason and seeing no prospect of fire given the torrential rain, probably headed to the Koroit Station for some lunch with the others. As I had already experienced, that would be better, that would be much better!

Upon reaching home soaked to the skin, the sun came out just as I headed in for a hot shower. Although the dream book said rat dreams can be about change, it said nothing about changeable weather.

16

Into the Light

It was pitch black on Tuesday morning at 6:00 a.m., the start of the working week after the long weekend. My usual departure time was 6:45, and with an important meeting at 9:00, there was nothing else for it but to leave in the pre-dawn. There were no lifts to work available, although the bus was always an option. When deciding back in January on how best to get to work, the bus didn't appeal. With the pandemic still causing uncertainty, sporadic lockdowns and COVID-19 outbreaks, the prospect of sitting on a bus with other unknown persons wasn't enticing. Vaccinations had commenced in Victoria, and very few live cases remained. Wearing a mask was still mandatory on public transport, so the bus seemed less risky.

However, I felt that taking the bus was still a bit of a cop-out. I had signed up to ride the bike to work as bad as it got, and I was determined to see it through to the end. A positive of the challenge was the resulting sense of achievement, so getting a lift or catching the bus was a last resort. Somewhat stubbornly, I chose to keep riding. Stubbornness is also a character trait of mine, which sometimes falls into the category of cutting off my nose despite my face.

Into the Light

It was quite eerie riding in the dark, but I knew I was riding into the light and that it would only be dark for about fifteen minutes of my journey. The bike was fitted with a small battery-powered light which gave off just enough light to see where I was going but not much else. I had considered getting a bigger, more powerful light but thought it was a waste of money as my ban would be over before it got really dark.

On this particular morning, that decision was questionable.

As I passed the sheep in the paddocks near home at the start of the ride, their eyes glowed strangely. Other animals, which I assumed were possums, grunted at me from the tree tops to ward me off. As far as I was aware, there were no reports of tree climbing pigs in Koroit, so possums it must be.

The other aspect of autumn apart from the shorter days and later sunrises was the fallen leaves, and there were many. I could easily identify them in the daylight, but they could be anything in the dark, and I approached with caution. Suddenly, a cat that was crouching by the roadside took fright and shot out in front of me. It was hard to tell who had had the biggest fright. Best not say what I said, but it was loud, rude and in old-fashioned English. I'm not superstitious, but I bet it was a black cat.

The other problem with night riding was that I usually wore sunglasses to protect my eyes from insects, and this was not an option in the dark. I considered clear glasses but dismissed them for the same reason as the more powerful light. Early mornings are not usually known for a lot of insects, but I certainly discovered the ones that were up early. *Whack!* A bug flew straight into my left eye, and it stung! I managed to finally remove the insect which had worked its way under my eyelid, and I resumed my journey. That was two reasons to have taken the bus! On reflection, however, it did vindicate my decision to not put a bigger light on the bike, as I didn't welcome the thought of attracting a moth or larger insects to my face.

The sky was lightening as I reached the rail trail, but it was still dark enough for my senses and awareness to stay sharp. The empty trail stretched out before me, so with determination and less speed than usual, my journey continued. I approached dark objects on the trail with caution and suspicion. A leaf dropped from a tree in front of me, which led to further profanity. Thinking it was a startled bird, I swerved wildly and into some long grass on the edge of the trail. The gradient down Tower Hill is enough to pick up quite a bit of speed without pedalling, and I was pelted by the weed tops as I ploughed through. The weeds along this section of the trail are particularly hardy, as you can imagine, and my trousers and socks collected burs and grass seeds in a sort of rusted-on fashion statement. It was a bit like people these days wearing jeans that are ripped. My mother would have had a fit! Perhaps I should leave the burs on as a new fashion. They were digging into me, so it seemed a good idea to stop and remove the prickly interlopers, fashion or not, and to have a break from the trauma of riding in the dark. I wondered if the nice bus driver would let me put my bike on the bus if I saw it. Then again, I didn't remember seeing it previously on my rides to work, so it was probably a wasted thought.

The sky was brightening into an overcast but still and dry day, thankfully. I reached the bottom of the hill and approached the road section of the trail through Illowa, which would be easier. The safer option on a dark, overcast morning was to avoid traffic, so I took the route through the wetlands rather than over the bridge. As I passed a ploughed field, there were literally hundreds of wild Cape Barren geese picking at whatever had been disturbed by the plough. They were beautiful birds with striking pink legs and grey speckled plumage.

Much of the trail in the wetland section is fine gravel, which needs to be traversed with care to avoid sliding off. In some parts of the wetland, the water is beside the trail—something I did not wish to add to my list of adventures. Despite having plenty of sick leave, catching a cold on a cool, wet ride of about ten kilometres was not my idea of a good start to the day. The wetlands are usually deserted in the morning, so it was unusual that I could see a vehicle approaching in the distance. It was a truck.

"What the…?"

I pulled off to the side in one of the few passing places and waited for it to pass. It showed no sign of slowing down and thundered past me showering me in fine gravel and splatterings of wet, slightly pungent essence of rail trail. Riding this morning in the dark and now gloomy morning was turning out to be up there with a number of bad decisions I had made in life, including calling the school bully a dickhead.

I finally made it to work late. I changed and washed in a hurry and made it to the meeting just as it started. A colleague gave me an odd sort of look, which I assumed meant that in my haste, I'd failed to remove all traces of rail trail from my face. The meeting went OK, but I was a bit flustered by the morning's events. I had a slight headache and made a mental note to look up the bus timetable.

I left later the next few days and avoided the darkness. It was an easier ride, and I ticked another week off the list. In addition to literally riding into the light, I was metaphorically riding into the light. For each passing day, my ban was gradually elapsing.

The house planning process also advanced. The planning permit for our new house in Port Fairy had been granted with the drawings approved and the builder scheduled to start the following month. This was exciting as we were keen to get the house built and move back to the coast. Not that living in Koroit was bad. In fact, we had made the change easily, and Koroit was quite lovely, and the mowers were growing on me, but we missed the ocean.

There was a new aspect of my life that came with not being allowed to drive: I enjoyed riding the bike into the village for day-to-day items. This was something I could see myself doing in addition to riding for fun and exercise on weekends when my ban was over.

It was a rainy Saturday morning again. Despite the day before being thirty degrees, the majority of the summer and autumn had certainly been wet and cool. The rain stopped around noon, so I headed out for a ride.

This time of year is pivotal in the Victoria sporting world. The cricket season is coming to an end and the football season beginning, so both sports are played at the same time.

Coming home from work past the recreation reserve, training for both sports was in full flow, one on each oval.

Koroit were playing a practice match. I knew it was a practice match, as their opponents were a team from Warrnambool from a different league, and entry was free. When my father was alive, he would wait until after half-time to go in whenever we went to a country football match, as the gate was not manned and entry was free! The scoreboard was also not in use, which may have been an act of kindness, as the visitors were clearly having the worst of it. The away team's supporters (and there was a decent crowd) didn't need to be reminded of the full horror of the score. One thing had certainly not changed: the Koroit boys were big!

A passing shower came through as I reached Koroit Station, so I decided to stop under the shelter and wait for it to pass. Out of the corner of my eye, I noticed a small surveillance camera pointing directly at the place I was standing. It was the first time I had noticed cameras at the station. Presumably, the cameras were installed to deter vandalism and graffiti, but who knows what other things they recorded. I waited under the eaves of the old goods shed and watched the rain slowly recede into the distance. The goods shed is quite secluded and sheltered away from the other buildings and the playground. I noticed a discarded remnant of an evening's passion. It seemed the old station was a spot for more than just picnics and playgrounds.

The increasing darkness of the mornings was problematic. Some days I had to be at work for an early start, and flexibility extended only so far. It looked like the bus might finally get a gig.

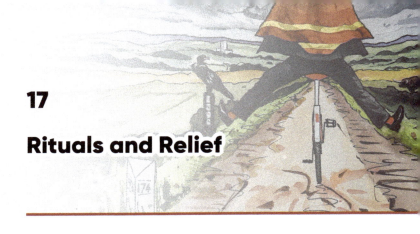

17

Rituals and Relief

With the month of March passing and the light in the early morning receding, I decided to take the bus. There were offers of a lift, but it always felt like I was imposing. Of course, I wouldn't have been at all, but that's how it felt, so I gave the bus a crack for a change and my earlier concerns easing with the health situation improving. There was the appealing challenge of seeing this thing through on the bike, and catching the bus was the easy way out, but it was necessary as a contingency.

The bus arrived, and we got off to a bad start.

"Concession?" the driver asked.

"Full fare," I hastily responded.

Did I look that old? Maybe riding to work and back had aged me or maybe I needed stop being so bloody vain and accept that I was reaching the age when I was entitled to a bus pass. When I recovered from the surprise of being asked for a concession fare, I decided that when I reached the eligibility age for a bus pass I wouldn't accept it!

We rattled and bumped our way to Warrnambool, which only took about twenty minutes. There were only three of us on the bus, and we were all wearing masks, which was still a requirement on public transport. It was a perfectly simple and cheap alternative, but a cop-out that would diminish my sense of achievement at the end.

The next day, I steeled myself for the bike to get this thing done! I set off for work in a stiff headwind that contained spits and spots of rain. The area is well-known for being windy, so it was not an enjoyable ride. Even many of the hard-core riders at work left their bikes at home.

The weather was much better the rest of the week, and I made it in and out without incident. By the weekend I was starting to believe that the challenge of commuting to work for three months was within my grasp.

I was asked to work on a day during my holidays, which meant I could exchange this day to start my holidays a day earlier. So there it was, just three days left to go. The weather forecast for the week was changeable, with heavy rain and strong winds predicted mid-week, perfect for riding to work and back!

Severe flooding was causing havoc in the north of the country, and there were hundreds of families evacuated and houses inundated up to the rooftops. We saw frightening images of cars and people being swept away in torrents of water, and lakes forming in the weirdest places. Victoria was due to cop the tail-end of this severe weather system, which perfectly lined up with my last few days of commuting. My three-month riding adventure was building up to a race to the line.

With a heavy day of critical meetings at work, I couldn't risk a fall or breakdown in the middle of nowhere, so I took the bus on Monday.

Just two to go.

On Tuesday, I got lucky and the weather held.

And then there was one. The forecast was grim for Wednesday, my last day. In case it was too dangerous I had arranged a contingency. There are several vans at work that are used for various things, and one of these was able to collect me in Dennington to drive me and the bike the remaining distance to work if I needed it. It was still a ride of some fifteen kilometres, so at least it was most of the way and eased some of my guilt. There was nothing worse than starting a long day with a cold, wet ride. My past experiences were not pleasant. So the plan was if I wanted a lift for the last bit, I should wait under the trees in Dennington at 8:00 a.m.

The early hours of the morning were still and dry, but as I was getting ready and loading up the bike, the wind started whistling and whining under the garage door. The rain came shortly after. It was too good to be true, it was right on cue! I packed some dry clothes thinking the final ride was building up to a crescendo! There was no reason why I had to ride, and I still had time to abort the mission and catch the bus, but it somehow cheapened everything I had accomplished over the previous three months. No, as bad as the weather was, I was absolutely determined to finish this off the way it started, so dammit I rode! With everything I had been through to get to this day—a day I had looked forward to so much—I did not want to win the challenge on a forfeit.

As I left home, the rain was light, and the wind was strong but bearable. It is deceptive in a built-up area as the buildings and trees can provide shelter from wind

Rituals and Relief

and rain. On the outskirts of town where there are no buildings or cover of any sort, the full force of the elements hit me. It was barely daylight, rather cold and a brutal wind drove the rain. With a song running through my head about a shipwreck on one of the great lakes and rain stinging my eyes and face, I pushed into it singing "In the face of a hurricane west wind!" E-bikes are quite fast, which accentuates the prevailing weather. Hot is hotter, winds are stronger—and rain?—rain is so much wetter and it penetrates more deeply. With only a raincoat, I was becoming thoroughly soaked to the skin.

The trail was deserted save for a few brave rabbits that scampered out of my way hurriedly (and with good reason; today I was on a mission!). Without a soul in sight, I wasn't afraid of embarrassing myself, so I started roaring the battle cry of a medieval army charging into battle. My feet were off the pedals stretched out triumphantly. Cold and wet, I raced down Tower Hill for the last time. I was quietly grateful that despite this foul blast, at least it didn't snow around here.

As I arrived at the bottom of the hill, I stopped under the shelter of some trees for a drink. With the amount of water lashing my face and body, I was surprised that I was so thirsty; my throat was dry from the roaring, I guess. I looked on enviously as cars in the distance made their way happily to wherever they were going. The occupants would be warm and dry, possibly enjoying some coffee, which was a far cry from being hammered by the wind and pressure washed by the rain. But it was entirely my choice to ride, so there was no point feeling hard done by.

This rain put me in mind of my long-suffering mother who had endured my childhood antics. She used to say, "If it was raining film stars, I'd get Lassie." She got it from a film she had seen. And this day it was certainly not raining film stars. It was raining rain! Mum and I shared a wicked sense of humour. One of our favourite jokes was stopping to pick some weeds from the roadside when I went to visit her for the weekend. I'd present her with the weeds instead of a bunch of flowers, which most normal sons would do. If she had company when I did this, people stared at us in amazement. She would take out a vase, pop the weeds in water and put them in pride of place. To complete the ridiculous charade, I would say, "I think a dog has peed on them."

"Oh Darling," Mum would say, "how lovely and thoughtful you are."

We would go on as if this was completely normal, with further strange looks from the guests. It is fair to say that our sense of humour was unwell, but it has served me quite well in life (except with police).

The rain was now horizontal, and I was thoroughly soaked through. The appeal of a lift for the last part was irresistible, so I waited and took it. When I arrived at work, I thanked my generous driver, changed into dry clothes—including a spare pair of shoes and socks this time—and got on with the day. My co-workers were amazed I had ridden again that morning, which probably confirmed their view of my questionable sanity. In Warrnambool, the weather that time of year was usually lovely, but it didn't stop raining that day.

It was dry at the end of the day, so I hastily set off. When I reached the outskirts of Warrnambool on my way home, Koroit, which was usually visible in the distance, was missing. In its place was a white, misty haze. Rain, and probably lots of it. The last ride was turning into a race. There were a few drops of rain and just a forlorn hope that it might stay dry enough to get home dry. A rider on a serious road bike came up behind me and said with a wry smile, "I think we are gunna get wet," and rode off ahead at twice my pace.

"Yeah maybe," I said, still clinging to the remote possibility that it was just mist.

But he was right. As I rode up the hill, the rain seriously set in. For the second time that day I was hopelessly in a deluge in the middle of the ride. The funny thing was, it was OK. It was my last commute, and although the rain was relentless, there was a hot shower at the end of it. Accepting your fate can be comforting in a weird sort of way. There was nothing else to do than just push on and get it done once and for all.

As I pedalled home, I mused about a time as a young guy living on my own in Ferntree Gully at the foot of the Dandenong Ranges. I was having a beer with two of my maddest mates one day, and we were complaining about how we'd all had rotten luck recently. We discussed the situation with some degree of gravity and decided that the only course of action was to conduct some sort of ritual to appease the spirits who were causing our collective misfortune. We pooled our ideas over further beers and decided a food effigy would do the trick. Pickings were sparse in the cupboards (mouldy bread, a few potatoes, limp broccoli) and fridge (beer and mayonnaise). My house was very much a bachelor pad, and this tasty assortment was not uncommon in those days.

We were in no state to drive, so these assorted offerings would have to do. But how to actually make the offering? We decided that the clothes line could work; at least it was vertical and we could hang the food from it. Perfect. We also decided that the spirits wouldn't drink beer so we kept that for ourselves. With the meagre foodstuffs suitably attached, we commenced chanting and ceremonially dancing around the clothesline.

"Bread, potato and broccoli; bread, potato and broccoli!"

Once we had made the point, we retired back inside the house to finish our beers. Out of nowhere, a black dog we had never seen before walked through the garden. In our alcohol-fuelled state we stared at each other incredulously. It was perfectly clear that the only explanation for this mysterious dog was that our ritual had worked and the evil that had befallen us was leaving in the form of the metaphor of the black dog. It had worked! Our luck would now surely be restored. The spirits were appeased. Apart from a bad hangover the next day, things seemed to improve. Smiling at this crazy time in my life, I wondered whether a repeat bread, potato and broccoli session would have changed my fate (or at least the weather) over the previous three months.

The Labradors were waiting by the gate as usual when I reached home. They, too, were sopping wet but were smiling at me and wagging their tails. It was nice to be home. I peeled off my wet clothes, immersed myself in a hot shower and washed away the day's events. It had been almost three months of riding to work including the few days that I rode when I was still able to drive at the beginning. The mad cow adventures, snakes, trucks and other perils were behind me, and I had done it. Feeling a bit chuffed with myself, I went outside to play "fetch the ball" with the dogs, content that I had done what I set out to do.

Although there were a few more weeks of riding around ahead of me, at least it was not a daily commute in all kinds of weather. I could please myself when I rode the bike, and a sense of relief washed over me like an autumn rain. I fed the dogs, sat down with a nice glass of wine and smiled inside.

Tomorrow was the March 25, my birthday.

18

Holidays

Hooray! Don't you just love that feeling when you start holidays? It's one of my most enduring of happy memories. It wasn't that I had anything spectacular planned. In fact, I had no plans whatsoever. I couldn't go anywhere without a car, and Jo was working, so my list of options was quite thin. But this year was very different. I had made it through some pretty challenging times. I was still on the bike for a few weeks, but with no day-to-day work pressures to worry about and no daily commute, the worst was over. As with everything in life, choosing to do something is so much better than having to do it!

With time on my hands during my first day of leisure, I decided to explore other parts of the area I hadn't yet. The weather was warm, so it seemed a good opportunity.

In the village, a guy resembling Captain Mainwaring from *Dad's Army* was striding along purposefully. As I was riding past, out of nowhere he stopped and said, "Keep riding, you look like you could use it!"

No way! I slowed down and said, "Speak for yourself ya fat bastard!"

He was so shocked he roared at me in indignation and seemed to think about chasing me. It was a good time to leave to avoid any further exchange of insults. This was a bit of a risky remark in the demerit points department and a bit cavalier in the small village I would be living in for some time yet, and one I may live to regret if we crossed paths again. He would certainly remember me. But then again thought if it happened, I'd be able to outrun him or take the Labradors with me who could lick him to death. If this kept up, building the house in Port Fairy—or better still, getting my licence back—was fast becoming a priority so I could avoid spontaneous outbursts of profanity in Koroit.

I was also being recognised more often. Two people had spoken to me as I rode past. "Hi Glenn" and "Morning Glenn" were becoming commonplace, which is what I had expected in the beginning. *Perhaps I should be a bit more careful in hurling insults at people in the future*, I thought. There was always the bad behaviour demerit points to consider as well. With only a few weeks to go, the last thing I needed was to fall off again or to get into an argument with a random stranger.

Men's football had resumed in the AFL on the previous weekend. Crowds were allowed back in limited numbers, and at least for the time being life was slowly returning to the pre-pandemic norm as the COVID-19 vaccine was rolled out. Active case numbers in Victoria were zero, at least for now, and were minimal in Australia as a whole. But I remained suspicious about this pandemic as parts of the world were really struggling, with countries such as the UK and USA going flat out to get their citizens vaccinated.

Being on holidays gave me time for reflection. It was a remarkable achievement to have invented a vaccine for the ghastly virus that had brought so much death and misery. To get it rolling in such a short time was a testament to human ingenuity. The coronavirus pandemic, despite the terrible consequences, had brought about some changes that were positive. Medical appointments could now be conducted remotely via telehealth as it was called. This was a huge advancement that saved time, travel and hassle. People could also work from home more easily because organisations seemed to trust their staff more. This meant less reliance on transport and commuting, and people could now live out of the city. This was huge. I also noticed that we seemed to band together as a community more. There was a real sense of helping each other, which I hoped would continue. So it wasn't all bad.

It was also a time to reflect on the past few months of my life and how it changed in the blink of an eye. The whole riding experience, including the pandemic, had taught me a few important things. Take nothing for granted, enjoy life, stay positive and try not to be rude to people. The latter, of course, was sometimes a challenge. Oh, and avoid speeding.

My first day of holidays was bright and sunny, if a bit breezy. As I rode along, I solved a mystery. Most of the garage doors along the way were shut, so I decided that leaving them up in summer was safe because there was no crime in the village, and the open doors must have provided ventilation against the relentless heat. I preferred the more fanciful theories that had occurred to me earlier, but ventilation was likely the answer.

For a change of scenery, I went down a few streets that I had not visited before. A murder of crows swore at me as I rode along a tree-lined street. If you have ever heard a crow, you will understand the swearword their cry resembles. I have always wondered why a flock of crows was called a murder. They're more like thieves than murderers. It seemed they were treated rather harshly in that regard.

The weather was a far cry from the week before but quite gusty, so I headed for home. I was almost at home when I came upon some roadwork, so I crossed onto the footpath to avoid it. An older couple were walking along ahead of me. The footpath was narrow, and they took up almost the entire width of it. Riding slowly behind them, I rang the bell to let them know I was approaching. Nothing. They didn't deviate. So I rang it again. Still nothing. So I got off and walked the bike between them.

"She won't hear ya," the chap said.

There would be advantages to having a wife or partner who was stone deaf, and they put me in mind of my grandfather who was also hard of hearing. He wasn't really my grandfather. I don't remember meeting my dad's father. He was the second husband of my grandmother, but we always referred to him as Pa. Pa was a typical old bushman who always wore a hat. He shaved with this terrifying cut-throat razor which he sharpened on a piece of leather he referred to as "The Strap." If I was ever cheeky, he would say, "I'll get the strap!" But he never did.

He was brilliant at fixing and making things, but he especially loved fishing. He taught me how to fish when I was very young, probably about five years old, I reckon. He would pick me up in his battered old truck and take me to a river, creek or the ocean. If there was a fish in any of those bodies of water, Pa would catch it. He could fly fish and surf fish. One day he caught a stingray, which he referred to as a "stingerray"! Thinking he had caught a nice big fish, he was most put out by the stingerray that fouled his reel when it took off.

"Bloody pest," he said.

Eels in the river were also referred to as "bloody pests". Our favourite fishing spot was in Allansford on the Hopkins River. He called the spot "the black hole of Calcutta," and there were plenty of fish to be had but also eels. Whenever he hooked something in that spot he would always say, "I bet ya it's a stinkin' eel!" He was invariably right. He could also tell what kind of fish he had hooked before he landed it and would say "Bream" before drawing it out of the water on the line.

He had his own sayings to use if I was naughty, which I often was. He'd say things like, "You'll go over," or "I'll put you in an Indian death lock or a Boston crab," (which I think were wrestling terms). These were fearsome terms to me as a boy and usually forced me to behave myself. He would also refer to me as a "cheeky possum."

Another "pest" stole his lunch one day. Dad was living up in the Dandenong's outside Melbourne in a place called Selby. It is a beautiful place in the bush that is famous for Puffy Billy, a restored steam engine which takes visitors on a short ride through the mountains. One

Sunday afternoon, Dad cooked steak and sausages over a wood fire. From out of nowhere, a Kookaburra flew down and pinched the steak off Pa's plate right out from under his hand. Pa was furious!

"Oi rude cheeky bird, bloody pest!" he shouted.

Of course in those days, nothing much was open on a Sunday, so Pa had to make do with the sausages. The kookaburra fared much better. We were great mates up until he died in his nineties.

Easter was early this year—of course it was, the Easter eggs had been on sale for months now. April 2 was Good Friday, and the weather was forecast to be thirty degrees. That'd be right, the weather was coming good just as I had stopped commuting to work in a blizzard. From my experience, Good Friday was anything but good. It means "holy" or "good" day, but it usually wasn't for me as a young guy. It was a day of almost torture. We were only allowed to eat Easter eggs on Easter Sunday, so the scrumptious eggs would stare at me tauntingly all through Good Friday. All we were allowed to eat was smelly fish all day. Mum was never much of a cook, and as with most households back then, food was served bland. Jamie Oliver nor many of the trendy television chefs of today were around to provide ideas and inspiration to parents who cooked. There was none of this crisp vegetable nonsense in Mum's day. She'd start boiling the sprouts in early December to make sure they were cooked enough for Christmas Day lunch.

Mum used to say Good Friday was a day of sacrifice, a symbolic gesture in reference to the crucifixion. Why was it called Good Friday? It didn't make sense to me. To add to the misery, nothing was on or open on Good Friday, which added to the boredom and injustice of staring at the Easter eggs all day. Things are very different these days. Many shops are open, and there is usually a lot for kids to do to stop them from getting up to mischief or setting fire to things out of boredom.

I rode into the village in the early morning on Good Friday to buy a coffee for Jo as I did on my days off. It was a hive of activity. The gates were locked at the rec reserve which I usually rode through. This was new. Cars were arriving, and it dawned on me: football season had started and Koroit were playing at home. I rode around the reserve rather than through it, and I noticed that Koroit were playing my old team, South Warrnambool. Probably a day of sacrifice for the South lads.

After breakfast and before it got too warm, I went for a ride to check out what was going on in Koroit on a Good Friday. As I rode down our street, a small procession was approaching. What was this? About twenty sombre-faced individuals were walking slowly with one of them carrying a large wooden cross. *Nice gesture*, I thought. It was something I had never seen before.

The other modern-day Good Friday tradition is the collection for the Royal Children's Hospital appeal to raise money to help sick kids in hospital. Whilst it's a very worthy cause, they use the fire brigade to collect money from people's houses door-to-door, and blaring sirens cry out for hours on end. This didn't happen when I was growing up, as the fire brigade would be needed to put out fires that the kids had started because they had nothing better to do on Good Friday.

I took to the serenity of the rail trail to escape the blaring sirens. It was deserted as I rode along past now familiar sights. It was a nice way to pass the time in the solitude of the Australian bush on a lovely warm morning in April. The Aussie bush has a wonderful fragrance, particularly after rains or on warm days such as this one. The eucalypts give off a pleasant scent apparently to ward off predatory insects. As I was admiring this, a wasp landed on my arm. It obviously thought I smelt better than the trees. I flicked it off before it could sting me and headed out from under the trees before this Good Friday would be remembered for a wasp sting in addition to boredom, no Easter eggs until Sunday and hours of sirens.

On the way back, I passed the rec reserve where the game was in full swing. I was too far away to read the scores on the scoreboard but could see that the home team had many more digits than the visitors. I stopped for a few minutes and watched Koroit score freely on poor old South. Yes, in a world of change there was a certain reassuring inevitability about playing Koroit at Koroit.

With car horns going off regularly with each goal (mainly at the Koroit end), the sirens starting to fade off into the distance. I headed for some peace and quiet, and fish and chips from Poppies, the local takeaway in Koroit. They do some great food, and it's where I get a morning coffee, but the fish and chips win it hands down for me. I've had some great fish and chips, including in Scotland which were very good, but Poppies is the best.

On Easter morning, as usual I rode into town for the paper and a coffee. Leaving my bike helmet on as I went in to Poppies, old mate behind the counter said, "Is that one of those motorised bikes?"

"Yes," I said. "I've been riding it to work in Warrnambool."

He just stared at me for a few seconds in apparent amazement, then said, "Stuff that."

And I had, at least for now.

I rode back through the deserted rec reserve, which was a far cry from the day when it was absolutely packed with people for the football. The local paper detailed the football scores from the previous day: Koroit 102, South Warrnambool 54. The headline read "Saints in Heaven." Koroit are called The Saints, and although a fitting headline for the Easter weekend, I imagined the game was anything but saintly, particularly for South.

With the promise of another warm day, I set off for my ride, which was now firmly ingrained in my lifestyle. An unintended consequence of losing my licence was that riding was now a way of life and definitely a change for the better. I'd heard stories of people in their 90s still riding around for exercise and saw evidence of this every weekend. Older folks would go for a ride, but, irritatingly, park in large numbers outside Poppies to buy at least six coffees each. Great for Poppies, but annoying for me to wait. Losing my licence had done nothing to improve my impatience.

I noticed a small plane flying quite low as I rode along, and it reminded me of a day not long ago when I was listening to the radio. People were phoning in telling stories about their experiences in fire situations. We had very little hot weather that summer so there hadn't been many fires, thank goodness. In the broadest of Aussie accents, this guy said he was on his farm where a fire was close by. There were fire trucks nearby, and he was checking to see how close the fire was in case he needed to get out of the area.

"Yeah well," he drawled slowly, "I was out in the paddock, and I could see this plane. I didn't really pay much attention to it, I was more, ya know watching the fires. Then, this siren goes off, and a door opens under the plane. The next thing I know, I'm covered in all this red shit!"

The radio presenter was laughing so much, and so was I. We really do find others' misfortune hilarious.

The plane I was watching flew off slowly into the distance and started to gradually descend as it approached the airport just outside Warrnambool. No doubt it was going to land at the end of its journey or maybe have a short stopover before setting off again. It was a fitting metaphor. My journey on the bike was ending, too, at least the serious stuff. There would always be the recreational component on evenings and weekends if the weather co-operated.

The other thing that ended over Easter was daylight saving. The clocks were put back to their natural time of day, days were getting shorter and nights longer in the inexorable passing of time before the cycle started all over again.

In my first week of holidays, the weather was lovely with warm sunny autumn days of around 30°C, perfect for recreational riding. By the weekend, the weather turned cold and windy. Autumn was turning into winter, or so it seemed after such a warm week. In between rain showers on Saturday morning, I used my battle-hardened riding skills to venture into town to get a coffee in the usual place. I had to time it so I could find shelter if I needed to between heavy showers.

"Geez you're dicing with it today riding in this weather!" the guy behind the counter said.

He must have been convinced that I was a deranged individual riding to work in Warrnambool and now in this weather. I was now such a regular customer, he started making my coffee as I was getting off the bike—a nice touch. It also could have been to avoid the risk of getting into a conversation with me. My sanity was in question, and there was a long day ahead of him. He must encounter all sorts.

I stopped here and there for shelter on the way home; it was no problem. The various sprinklers at the footy ground were still left on from the warm weather. The wind was blowing the water well over the path, so it was a test of timing to avoid getting rained on and soaked by a blast from the sprinklers at the same time. How does the saying go? If they don't get you on the roundabout, they'll get you on the swing.

With the month of April nearly done, the three months had passed. A chapter of my life was closing, and a new one was about to be written. Change is good. Some people don't like change, which I can understand and there can be changes for the worst, but in this case change was definitely good.

April 20, 2021 was the last day of enforced riding. It was a cold, wet morning, a fitting end to the three months spent on the bike. My work car I usually drove was being delivered that afternoon in readiness for me to drive it again the next day. Once the rain had stopped there was just a cold wind blowing as I rode into town to buy some lunch. Coming out of the shop, I heard a loud voice call out, "G'day Glenn!" It was becoming more common that locals would stop to chat as I went about my daily affairs. It was our landlord's father who also lived in Koroit and would mow the lawns of our rented property that his son owned. We had become quite good friends chatting about this and that whenever he came to mow. Our dogs, who were initially suspicious of him when he arrived to start the ride-on mower (of course), barked madly at the gate, but after a while they tried to encourage him to throw the ball for them. It became a regular game.

The other thing that was becoming regular were these chance encounters with people we had come to know while living in Koroit. In order to be considered local, you not only had to be living there—that alone didn't qualify—you had to have been born there. Then you were only just local. True locals were descended from generations of Koroitonians (if that's what they are called), but having a chat now meant I was probably on a visitor's visa, and that was good enough. It was nice to be accepted into the community nonetheless.

"Nice drop of rain," he said. "I was gonna come over and mow the lawns this arvo, but it's a bit wet."

"Just a tad," I responded. "Hey, I get my ticket back tomorrow!"

He smiled and said, "I'll bet you'll be glad about that."

"Yes, but I'll still ride the bike to do bits of shopping like this."

"Yeah," he said emphatically. "It's not far, just down the hill."

I always locked my bike, so when I went to unlock it he said, "Need to lock the bike in Koroit?"

"Nah," I said. "I just don't want to walk back if it gets pinched."

He laughed and said, "I'll come to mow on Friday."

In a complicated world with all that was going on, the simplicity of being recognised and having a pleasant chat is something I love about living in a community, if only on a "visitor's visa."

I rode home to beat the rain thinking about how inconvenient being without a car can be. Of course, this is what the penalty was intended to do—cause inconvenience to teach me a lesson. Apart from the obvious loss of liberty, one had to plan the journey, factor in the weather and dress in appropriate clothing, etc. I had learnt many lessons over the three months, including understanding my own limitations. But probably the most important lesson was not giving up and coping with adversity. In the scheme of things, losing my licence wasn't catastrophic, but it was a challenge to overcome and a chance to turn adversity into something positive. It was a bit like discovering penicillin from mould and X-rays with a scientific experiment that went wrong. I was thankful I hadn't required either of these during my time on the bike.

I hung the helmet over the handlebars and put the bike on charge for another day when I arrived home. It was pretty mud-splattered and had suffered a few months of coffee and other marks on it from the bumps in the road. We had certainly had some adventures together, some scrapes, near misses and near disasters. But we made through intact, if not both a bit battered and stained.

I was certainly fitter, had learned a few lessons and seen some bits of life I never would have unless I hadn't taken to the streets and the rail trail on a bike. I can thoroughly recommend it, but perhaps do it without the drama of getting an early Christmas present in the form of a three-month driving ban from the police.

The pandemic appeared to be easing. The awful disruption, and grief it brought with it, at least in Australia, seemed to be slowly receding. There were still COVID-19 spot fires in Australia popping up every now and then, unlike some countries which were still being ravaged by the disease, but thankfully, the pandemic in was under control in our part of the world. I had no idea if there would be more serious outbreaks or lockdowns in the future, but I had managed to get through unscathed to date. Although I had not received my vaccination yet and there was uncertainty over when that would be, I felt more optimistic.

As I walked in the door from the garage, Jo was listening to a song about all things passing, which perfectly fit how I felt at that moment. And the song felt so right. I would get my licence back tomorrow.

19

Done and Dusted

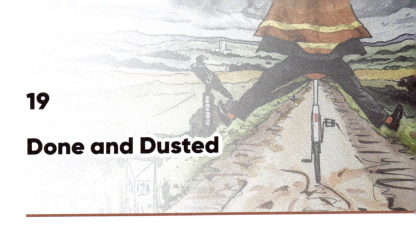

My suspension expired at midnight on the April 20, 2021. Why midnight for heaven's sake? But midnight it was. I had no plans to go for a drive in the middle of the night just to prove a point.

So exactly three months after surrendering my licence, I drove to VicRoads in Warrnambool to collect it. I found out it is legal to drive once the suspension was served, and I only needed to carry identification, so I could drive myself there and back.

I'd never surrendered my licence before, so I was not sure how easy or difficult it might be to get it back. Did they keep it in a safe somewhere and simply hand it back? Or was there some further rigmarole to go through? The letter I had been sent didn't say anything about the process to regain it, so I supposed I would find out soon enough.

Getting into the driver's seat for the first time in a while felt strange, and I was actually a bit nervous. I started the engine, adjusted the mirrors, plugged my phone in to charge, took a deep breath and backed out of the driveway for the first time in what seemed like ages. I felt a funny sense of something like guilt about driving. I couldn't put my finger on it; I felt I was somehow doing something wrong, and I had to reassure myself that I wasn't.

I drove into the village to get some breakfast on the way, and the radio news talked about the verdict in the George Floyd murder case in the United States. Former police officer Derek Chauvin had been found guilty of Floyd's murder. It was understandably the talk of the day as I drove along. My little battle with adversity paled in comparison. Interestingly, the date I handed in my licence, January 20, 2021, was the day that President Biden was inaugurated as the forty-sixth president of the United States. It certainly put some perspective around the significance of my last three months, but the end of my little chapter was still personally very significant.

I would certainly remember the two key dates in this whole affair which just happened on important dates in world history. It was a bit like when people would ask where you were and what you were doing on the day John Lennon died (for those old enough to remember) or the 9/11 collapse of the twin towers in New York.

I drove to Warrnambool at least five kilometres per hour BELOW the speed limits. I passed many of the parts of the rail trail that you can see from the road and reminisced about the many days in the all kinds of weather I had toiled along this journey. Was it really over? Reality hadn't quite sunk in yet.

I arrived at VicRoads at 8:30 a.m., the scheduled opening time, and there was already a queue outside the door. Awesome. I took a number and waited to be called. I waited and waited. It seemed like ages since I had given my licence up because of how much had happened in the past three months. I was a young man when all of this started!

The date on the little notice board read: Tuesday, April 20. My heart froze. You know that feeling you get when you lose track of what day it is when you're on holidays? Was I a day early? Had I driven in illegally? I had left my phone in the car so had no immediate way of checking the date. I pulled myself together and realised, no, it was bloody Wednesday the twenty-first! They had forgotten to put up the correct day and date. Nobody but me would have noticed the irony of the situation or seen the palpable sense of relief that came over me.

The same lady that served me when I surrendered my ticket greeted me with the same expression of indifference she had before. Was I just another number? Probably. No different to registering a boat trailer, a change of address or any of the other administrative functions that made up the working week. She must have dealt with hundreds of licence reinstatements, and it was just another process.

For me, it was anything but.

"How can I help?" she asked politely.

With the office now filled to its COVID-19-restricted capacity of seventeen people, there was quite an audience of onlookers who were all listening intently to each person being served probably to pass the boredom of waiting. This office must be the only place in the entire world that did not have a screen or television to keep customers amused. I handed her the notice I had received confirming the dates of my driving ban.

"I've been suspended for driving for three months for speeding, and I have come to get my licence back," I said in a low voice so as not to draw attention to the fact that I was a "criminal" in the eyes of the riveted onlookers.

"Pardon?" she said loudly.

I repeated in a louder voice.

"Speeding was it?"

Great! Now everyone would have heard it. I sheepishly turned around to see all eyes fixed on me!

Clearly now the centre of attention, she said, "Have you got your driver's licence there?"

I stared at her in amazement. Composing myself in front of the audience, I said, "No, I was told I had to surrender it so no I don't have my licence with me", I said trying to hide my utter amazement. Plastered all over the paperwork of the notice of suspension was the absolute requirement to hand in your licence to the very office I was standing in!

"Oh right," she said. "Have you got any other form of identification, like a credit card?"

"Yes, I have a brand new one," I said.

I instantly regretted it fearing that she may suspect this was some sort of identity fraud. But she was completely unfazed and started tapping away at her computer.

"I'll print you a paper licence and your new one will come in the mail," she said with a very discreet smile of understanding.

Although this was just another process in the vastness of government bureaucracy, she could see what returning my licence meant to me. This transaction seemed to be one of the nicer ones for her. I had been dreaming about it to the limit of my impatience and counting the days down one by one. Being able to drive is something that most of us take for granted. As with other things which are lost or taken away, it is only when we lose something that we can truly appreciate its value.

Almost everyone was staring at me as I walked out with my piece of paper, but I didn't care. It was done. I was officially legal again. With the way news spread around here, most people I knew would already know even before I told them I had my licence back!

Walking out of VicRoads reminded me of the many television programs I had seen over the years when prisoners were released from prison with a brown paper bag containing their worldly possessions. I was, of course, now a criminal with a driving conviction, so I should have brought a brown paper bag tied up with string to complete the theatre of it.

I felt a huge sense of relief driving home. I turned on the radio, cranked up the volume and sang along happily.

You know how in some thriller movies where they lure you into believing that whatever the horror the poor victims had endured was over and the movie would reach a happy conclusion only for a sudden final twist? Well, this tale had one more twist.

When I got home, I changed my clothes and poured a well-earned coffee. Phew! I felt my back pocket for my wallet, and it wasn't there. *Must have left it in the car*, I thought. I searched the car high and low. Nothing. Checked the bedroom, nup. I searched every room in the house, garage, garden, but came up with nada, zilch!

Not again!!

There was only one place it could be... Yep, VicRoads. It had to be. I had it last when I produced my credit card as identification. Damn and blast. In my eagerness to get the whole thing done, I must have been distracted!

There was nothing else for it. I reluctantly drove back to VicRoads in the hopes of retrieving my wallet. The thought of losing it again and going through all the drama and inconvenience of cancelling and reordering cards was unbearable. Not to mention the embarrassment of having to tell Jo that I'd lost my wallet such a short time after losing it (or not losing it, as was the case). It just didn't bear thinking about. It had to be at VicRoads. Please, pretty please...

When I arrived back at their offices, the queue was ten deep! I took another number so as not to upset anybody who thought I might be queue jumping. Whilst most Australians hate queuing up for things, we still meticulously observe the etiquette, and there was some pretty big blokes in the queue who might take umbrage. I waited for almost an hour before I was finally called. I asked if my wallet had been left behind that morning. Fortunately, the same nice lady served me. She was quite concerned and said, "No, I'm sorry. There is nothing here."

What on earth have I done to deserve this measure of bad luck? I thought. This was supposed to be a great day—a day I had been longing for—and now the shine was definitely coming off it.

As I drove home I really hoped I had mislaid it at home, but I felt a sense of despondency. I retraced my steps at home and was losing hope with every place my wallet wasn't. My last hope was the bedroom. And there, out of the corner of my eye, I saw it! It had somehow slipped behind the mattress on the bed. It must have happened when I got changed. Eureka!

"Aaah!" I cried suddenly.

Thank heavens. I almost wept with relief. Clearly, my confidence and concentration was affected by everything that had happened! But there was a pattern. My father used to vehemently say, "That was because you didn't concentrate!" when I did something clumsy or stupid. He was invariably right. I needed to have a good hard look at myself. I gave myself a swift telling off.

"Reddick, what has to happen before you begin to start learning from all of this?"

Finding my wallet was such a relief, and now I could just come and go as I pleased without worrying about the damn weather, getting knocked off and all of the other rigmarole. Driving into the village to pick up some groceries was a luxury. When I arrived at home, the dogs came racing to the gate barking furiously at this apparent stranger arriving in a strange car. They were accustomed to seeing me come and go on the bike. When they realised it was me they smiled and wagged their tails. Things had changed.

That night when Jo came home from work, I told her what had happened. She was not the least bit surprised, which reinforced my resolve. I really needed to concentrate more, stop being so impatient and stop rushing things. She gave me a hug, and we both laughed so much that the Labradors looked up at us in unison curiously with their heads tilted to one side.

As I reflected on the important things that had happened in my life, I decided everything happens for a reason. I recalled some of the many things I really wanted to happen at the time. After they didn't, I often looked back thinking, *Thank goodness that didn't happen!* There were other things that had happened that I didn't want, but my life actually turned out for the better. In the mood for reflection, I remembered an excerpt of a prayer I once saw. It said, "God grant me the serenity to accept the things that I cannot change, the courage to change the things I can, and the wisdom to know the difference."

The challenges over the previous three months must have been for a reason. I needed to change. I would make this experience the catalyst for my change. In the true spirit of the prayer, I made a series of "change" promises to myself to try to change a few aspects of my life. In the spring when the weather was good, I would try to ride to work occasionally. I owed this to myself in deference to what I had achieved and as a reminder of the privilege of being able to drive. I decided I must resist random outbursts of rudeness to strangers and to slow down and concentrate more on everything from now on.

COVID-19 and riding everywhere taught me to appreciate every day of my life. They taught me to appreciate and be thankful for the little things, the beauty of nature, the seasons and how lucky I really was. Now that travel restrictions had eased, I wondered if I should contact the boys in Melbourne to do another bread, potato, broccoli session just in case. For good measure.

On the weekend, I kept a promise to myself. Instead of driving to get the paper and the morning coffee, I took the bike. And I would do this now whenever I could. As I rode back with a coffee in the holder and the newspaper in the saddlebag, a chap was walking his dog.

"That's the way to do it!" he said.

"It is!" I said with a smile.

Something else important happened that morning. I received a phone call from our builder. He was ready to start our new house.

Change is good.

References

References used in writing this book include:

- The Port Fairy Warrnambool Rail Trail website and interpretive signage
- The Parks Victoria website
- Interestingengineering.com
- The Moyjil website

CPSIA information can be obtained
at www.ICGtesting.com
Printed in the USA
LVHW071007030821
694404LV00018B/1095